THE LIVERPOOL AND NORTH WALES STEAMSHIP COMPANY

John Shepherd

Ships in Focus Publications

Published in the UK in 2006 by Ships in Focus Publications,
18 Franklands, Longton
Preston PR4 5PD

Printed by Amadeus Press Ltd., Cleckheaton, Yorkshire.
ISBN 1 901703 67 3

Cover design by Paul Boot from an original poster painting by Samuel John Milton Brown, courtesy of Paul Kirkbride.
Above: *St. Tudno* at Llandudno early in the 1962 season, the last year of operations. *[Malcolm McRonald]*

FOREWORD

Over a period of more than 70 years the excursion sailings by the ships of the Liverpool and North Wales Steamship Co. Ltd. brought pleasure to generations of people from Merseyside, the North West of England, North Wales and further afield. The departure at 10.45 am of the 'Llandudno boat', and her return around 7.40 pm, were daily features at Liverpool's Pier Head in the summer months between Whitsun and mid-September.

My first sailing on a 'North Wales boat' took place when I was about nine years old. A visiting maiden aunt decided to take my brother and me for a day's outing to Llandudno. Later, our family became frequent Saturday or Sunday passengers, and it was a particular pleasure to return on the *St. Seiriol* at the later time of 6.30 pm. The *St. Tudno* was a lively vessel in any sort of sea other than flat calm. The water thrown up over her bow sometimes travelled well along the boat deck, so I quickly learned the spots to be avoided on rough days. We visited Colwyn Bay each year for our summer holiday, and occasionally sailed to Llandudno to get there. The highlight of one of these holidays was a day excursion to the Isle of Man on the *St. Seiriol*. This was my first visit to the island, and the first of my two Isle of Man sailings on that ship. For several years from the late 1950s, I held a 'twenty-trip ticket', and usually stayed on board to enjoy the sailing through the Menai Strait. I was on the *St. Tudno's* last sailing, when we all feared for her future. Next morning, I started work in Liverpool, and walked along the landing stage to my new office, passing the *St. Tudno* at her North Wales berth. It was the last time I ever saw her in the river. The announcement that the company was to cease trading came as a shock, but not a surprise, as the writing had been on the wall ever since the announcement that the *St. Seiriol* would not sail in 1962.

I sometimes wonder if things could have worked out differently. All steamer operators were suffering from the growth of the private car, but the Liverpool and North Wales company succumbed much earlier than those in other parts of the country. The management of the company gave the impression of being reluctant to face the need for change. As passenger numbers declined, two large ships had become an unaffordable luxury, especially when three of the *St. Seiriol's* six sailings each week were afternoon ones at a reduced fare. If the *St. Tudno* had been withdrawn a few years earlier, leaving the *St. Seiriol* to operate a reduced Liverpool to Llandudno service together with her Llandudno to the Isle of Man sailings, the company would certainly have lasted for at least a few more years. Better use could also have been made of the *St. Trillo*, as P. and A. Campbell proved when they took her over in 1963.

I am sure that all those people who have enjoyed excursion sailings to North Wales, by the Liverpool and North Wales Company's steamers, by Isle of Man steamers, or recently by the *Waverley* and *Balmoral*, will welcome John Shepherd's account of the company. This book will bring back many happy memories.

Malcolm McRonald

St. Seiriol. [Author's collection]

CONTENTS

St. Trillo in the Menai Straits on 25th August 1962.*[Malcolm McRonald]*

ACKNOWLEDGEMENTS

I am grateful for the assistance of David Docherty and Malcolm McRonald who have both proof read the original draft text for this book. Both these experts on the North Wales steamer services made various corrections, alterations and suggestions to my draft text, and these have been incorporated into the final version. Thanks very much to both these gentlemen for their time and interest.

The publishers would especially like to thank Ken Saunders, without whose superb collection of photos and ephemera the illustrative content of this book would be much poorer. Ken made only a few trips on the steamers to North Wales, but these were sufficient to kindle a lifelong interest in collecting material relating to the Liverpool and North Wales Steamship Co. Ltd. Thank you, Ken for being so generous in sharing your treasures. Thanks also to Clive Guthrie for help with details of the fleet list, to Louis Loughran for illustrations of flags and funnels, and for their help in finding photographs Tony Smith of the World Ship Society Ltd., Ambrose Greenway, F.W. Hawks and staff of the National Maritime Museum and Imperial War Museum.

John Shepherd.

St. Trillo leaving Llandudno Pier on 16th September 1962. Flying the flags always flown on the last departure of the season this transpired to be the last Liverpool and North Wales Steamship Company sailing. *[Malcolm McRonald]*

3

La Marguerite, approaching Menai Bridge by the late John Nicholson.

4

THE LIVERPOOL AND NORTH WALES STEAMSHIP COMPANY

Early days on the North Wales coast

The first known steam vessel plying between Liverpool and North Wales was a small paddle steamer, 90 feet in length, named *Cambria*. She was launched on 17th May 1821 and ran from Liverpool to Bagillt, on the Welsh side of the Dee estuary. The following summer saw the introduction of the first steamer link between Liverpool and the Menai Strait when the *Albion*, a slightly larger version of the *Cambria*, was placed on the route.

The first steamship company of any note to operate sailings from Liverpool to North Wales was the St. George Steam Packet Company, founded in 1821. A sailing bill dated 1824 states that its steamers *Prince Llewelyn* and *St. David* sailed regularly from George's Dock, Liverpool for Beaumaris and Bangor.

On 19th August 1831 the steamer *Rothsay Castle* was wrecked, with great loss of life, on the Dutchman's Bank at the entrance to the Menai Strait. Built in 1816 for service on the Clyde but not registered until 1821, the *Rothsay Castle* was quite unsuitable for the heavy weather which can be encountered in the Irish Sea. Although a full north westerly gale blew up on 18th August 1831, the *Rothsay Castle* left Liverpool at 10.15 am and ten hours later had only reached a point off the Little Orme's Head at Llandudno. So much water had found its way into the engine room that the coal was soaked and the fires could not be fed. Steam could not be maintained and the ship made less way than ever.

In the early hours of 19th August the *Rothsay Castle* struck the Dutchman's Bank. The ship carried no signalling apparatus, lights or gun to attract attention. The first signs of wreckage were seen at Beaumaris at about 6.00 am and the lifeboat was launched. Just twenty three passengers out of an estimated one hundred and forty on board survived the disaster. When the lifeboat found them many of the survivors were clinging to the ship's poop which was drifting towards Penmaenmawr. Those who had attempted to swim to nearby Puffin Island were all drowned. The *Rothsay Castle* tragedy led to the construction of Penmon Lighthouse to mark the channel between Puffin Island and Anglesey.

On 15th April 1843 the City of Dublin Steam Packet Company took over the North Wales passenger and cargo

Prince Arthur, an early steamer on the North Wales coast.
[J. & M. Clarkson collection]

business from the St. George Company and placed its steamer *Erin-Go-Bragh* on the service. This vessel had been built two years earlier for service on the River Shannon from Limerick. She was followed by the paddle steamers *Fairy*, *Prince of Wales* and *Prince Arthur*.

Many small companies operated along the North Wales coast in the mid-nineteenth century. Extensive research has been carried out into this period and can be found in Duckworth and Langmuir's 'West Coast Steamers' and F.C. Thornley's 'Steamers of North Wales'.

The completion of the railway along the North Wales coast in 1848 helped to popularise the coastal resorts even further, but it also brought stiff competition to the steamer companies, who thus far had had things all their own way. The coming of the railway was welcomed by many, as the ships had received scathing criticism in the local press regarding cleanliness and the general comfort of passengers.

In an effort to improve matters a new company, the Liverpool, Llandudno and Welsh Coast Steamboat Co. Ltd. was incorporated on 11th March 1881 with a nominal capital of £30,000. Its objective, as stated in its prospectus, was 'to provide improved passenger steamboat communications between Liverpool and the Welsh Coast'. The new company recognised that the key requirement for success was a fast, modern steamer. It chose the *Bonnie Doon*, which had been built in 1876 for the Glasgow to Ayr trade. She was, by the standards of the day, a modern ship, with a deck saloon for the use of first class passengers, a good turn of speed, and a robust construction designed for the exposed waters of the outer Firth of Clyde. Most important of all, she was being offered for sale, as she could no longer compete with the railway services on her designed route.

The sale of the *Bonnie Doon* to her new owners was registered on 21st April 1881, and her inaugural sailing along the North Wales coast took place just two days later on 23rd April. She was advertised to leave Bangor at 6.45 am, call at Beaumaris at 7.00 am, Llandudno at 8.00 am, and then on to Liverpool. The return sailing left Liverpool at 4.00 pm on weekdays and 1.30 pm on Saturdays. There was no Sunday service. The *Bonnie Doon* catered for passengers who required transport to and from North Wales and there was no provision

Bonnie Doon. [World Ship Society Limited]

but became more stable - if a little more pedestrian - during the second half of the decade. By 1889, as a result of better management, the company had returned to financial stability.

Formation of the Liverpool and North Wales Steamship Company

An important transitional stage in the history of the Liverpool to North Wales steamer services occurred in 1890. At that time the Fairfield Shipbuilding and Engineering Co. Ltd. of Govan had on its hands two paddle steamers, the *Paris* and the *Cobra*. The *Paris* had been built in 1875 by John Elder and Company of Govan - as the Fairfield Company was then known - for the London, Brighton and South Coast Railway and had been placed on its Newhaven to Dieppe service. She proved too slow for cross-Channel work and alterations made to her paddles brought little improvement in speed. In 1888 the *Paris* was sold back to her builders in part exchange for a new and faster ship. Fairfield reboilered and reconditioned her for service somewhere else - but where?

The *Cobra*, built by Fairfield in 1889, was designed to open a daylight service between the Clyde and Belfast for G. and J. Burns. She ran for a single season before being returned to her builders as unsatisfactory - and so Fairfield had two steamers on its hands, and no place for them to go. Like others before them who had tonnage they did not know what to do with, Fairfield thought of the North Wales service. Accordingly the New North Wales Steamship Company was formed and the two ships were registered in the name of Richard Barnwell, the managing director of the Fairfield company. The *Cobra* was renamed *St. Tudno* and ran the daily excursion sailing from Liverpool to the North Wales coast, whilst the much older *Paris* provided some weekend sailings for the newly formed company. A report in the

for the day excursion traffic which was left to the Liverpool tug owners, principally W. and T. Jolliffe.

The *Bonnie Doon* was running in opposition to the City of Dublin Steam Packet Company's three ageing steamers, but on 19th July 1881 an agreement was reached whereby the Liverpool, Llandudno and Welsh Coast Steamboat Company took over the City of Dublin's trade along the North Wales coast and acquired their steamers *Prince Arthur*, *Prince of Wales* and *Fairy*. The price for this was £17,500; £7,500 in cash and two thousand £5 shares in the new company. However, the *Fairy* was broken up before the end of 1881, the *Prince of Wales* was worn out, and the *Prince Arthur*'s passenger facilities were hopelessly outdated. Following the acquisition of the City of Dublin Steam Packet Company's steamers, the *Bonnie Doon* pioneered the daily excursion service from the Mersey to the Menai Strait. July 1881 is thus a key date in the history of the North Wales services for it marks the transition from a 'packet-boat' service to an 'excursion' service.

In early 1882 a new steamer was under construction at Rutherglen for North Wales services, the *Bonnie Princess*. At the end of June 1882 the *Bonnie Doon* returned to the Clyde, having been bought by Alexander Campbell of Rothesay. The delivery of the new *Bonnie Princess* was seriously delayed and it was left to the two old City of Dublin steamers to maintain a semblance of service. The new ship was much slower than had been advertised and in August 1882 it was reported that she had been replaced by a Liverpool tug whilst repairs were carried out.

The Liverpool, Llandudno and Welsh Coast Steamboat Company struggled on during the first part of the 1880s,

Bonnie Princess. [National Maritime Museum, London, Ref.5761]

'Llandudno Advertiser' dated 9th August 1890 stated: 'The *Paris* grounded off Beaumaris on her early morning sailing to Liverpool and it was late at night before she could be refloated and restarted. Fortunately for all, Mr. Barlow, the energetic secretary of the company, was at Beaumaris and did his very best to prevent inconvenience to the passengers.'

After only one summer of competition (1890) from the New North Wales Steamship Company, the Liverpool, Llandudno and Welsh Coast Steamboat Co. Ltd. went into liquidation and a new company, the Liverpool and North Wales Steamship Co. Ltd., was registered on 19th January 1891 to replace the two rival concerns of the previous year. This was

Cobra in the Clyde. *[Glasgow University Archives]*

explained in a prospectus issued to the public dated 21st February 1891 which stated that during the 1890 summer season the three steamers *St. Tudno (ex Cobra), Bonnie Princess* and *Prince Arthur* had carried over 214,000 passengers. The whole of the goodwill, property and assets of the Liverpool, Llandudno and Welsh Coast Steamboat Co. Ltd., including the lease of the pier at Menai Bridge, had been acquired by the new company on what were considered very moderate terms. The two well-known ships, *Bonnie Princess* and the *Prince Arthur,* which had been sailing for the old company for many years, had been acquired. In fact, *Prince Arthur* was never taken over. To replace the *St. Tudno,* a new ship had been ordered from Fairfield, who itself would become a large shareholder in the new company.

Early years of the Liverpool and North Wales company
The new ship referred to in the prospectus was launched in

April 1891 and given the name *St. Tudno*. Trials were run on 4th May and she achieved 20.4 knots, whilst on her voyage from the Clyde to Liverpool she averaged 19 knots. The new *St. Tudno* had accommodation for 1,061 passengers. A handbill for the 1891 season lists the Liverpool to Menai Bridge fare as 8/- (40p) saloon, 5/- (25p) steerage.

The *St. Tudno* was always a heavy burner of coal, consuming six or seven tons per hour. In 1891 bunker coal at Liverpool was 4/6d (23p) a ton, but the price was constantly rising. The *St. Tudno* lasted for 22 summers on the North Wales service. She made occasional trips to the Isle of Man from Llandudno, and in July 1907 she was scheduled to make three trips from Liverpool around Anglesey for a fare of 7/6d (38p) saloon and 5/- (25p) steerage. It was also usual for the *St. Tudno* to make a special sailing to Bardsey Island once a year leaving Liverpool at 8.00 am and returning at 10.00 pm, including a call at Llandudno. For several seasons she left

St. Tudno passing Bull Bay, Anglesey. *[K.C. Saunders collection]*

Menai Bridge and Llandudno early on Monday mornings, enabling Liverpool businessmen and merchants to be back in the city for the 10.00 am opening of markets and exchanges.

At the end of the 1912 season the steamer was sold to the Hamburg-Amerika Line and registered in the name of the MacIver Steamship Co. Ltd. for use as a tender at Southampton. In September 1914 the *St. Tudno* was taken over by the British Government and used as a tender to troop transports arriving at Spithead and the Solent. She herself became a troop transport in the Channel from 1916 until 1919 and then was laid up until 1922 when she was sold to the Dutch shipbreaker T.C. Pas.

The new *St. Tudno*'s running mate in 1891 was the *Bonnie Princess*, taken over from the Liverpool, Llandudno and Welsh Coast Steamboat Company. She had a passenger capacity of 620 and a speed of 14 knots.

By 1895 the Liverpool and North Wales Steamship Company had decided to dispose of the *Bonnie Princess* and to build a faster passenger steamer that would be more economical to run. She was sold after the 1895 season to the Hastings, St. Leonards and Eastbourne Steamboat Company. The *Bonnie Princess* left the Mersey for the last time on 27th May 1896 but her life on the south coast was short - in 1899 her owners were listed as the shipbreakers T.C. Pas of Holland.

A new ship for the new company: the *St. Elvies* of 1896

After the sale of the *Bonnie Princess* in 1895, services were improved by the addition of the larger and faster *St. Elvies*, a handsome two-funnelled, two-masted paddle steamer built by the Fairfield Shipbuilding and Engineering Company. She looked like a junior version of the *St. Tudno*, with her funnels not quite so widely spaced. The *St. Elvies* was launched on 13th April 1896 and became one of the most useful and hardest-worked ships which the company ever owned. On trials the *St. Elvies* attained almost 20 knots, and she had a service speed of 18.5 knots. By the Whitsuntide of 1896 she was ready for her maiden voyage.

The original funnels were rather short and painted yellow with black tops; but to give improved draught and to cope with the smut nuisance, a taller pair, painted yellow, was fitted in 1899. The *St. Elvies'* bridge was placed amidships, between the paddle boxes, until it was moved forward during a 1910-11 refit. The passenger capacity was 991 (compared with the *St. Tudno*'s 1,061), and she burned only half the

Standing room only - *St. Tudno* around the turn on the century. *[K.C. Saunders collection]*

Crowded again, but on this occasion with soldiers as *St. Tudno* and *Nenette* transfer them to the White Star Line's *Celtic* (20,904/1901) at Brest, France, on 25th January 1919. *[Imperial War Museum Q70019]*

amount of coal of the *St. Tudno*. The *St. Elvies* had a varied roster, including the Friday Liverpool to Menai Bridge service, and half-day sailings to Llandudno and occasionally to Blackpool, trips from Llandudno to Douglas and sailings 'Round the Isle of Anglesey'.

Early in her career the *St. Elvies* was involved in the only mishap of consequence in the history of the Liverpool and North Wales Steamship Company. On 19th September 1896, while outward bound to Llandudno on a Saturday afternoon excursion with about 250 passengers, she came into violent collision with the tug-excursion steamer *Hercules*,

SPLENDID SEA EXCURSION.

Tuesday, September 15, 1903,

(Weather and circumstances permitting,) by the Splendid Saloon
Paddle Steamer

"ST. ELVIES,"

ROUND THE ISLAND OF ANGLESEY

Leaving LIVERPOOL at 9-15 a.m. prompt.

☞ On this day Steamer does not call at any of the intermediate Stations, but proceeds direct past Llandudno, through the Menai Straits, going under the Suspension and Tubular Bridges, and passes Carnarvon about 1-30 p.m., South Stack (Holyhead) about 3-0 p.m., and arrives back in Liverpool about 8-0 p.m.

170 MILES SAIL.   DELIGHTFUL COAST SCENERY.

FARE—

	1st Saloon	2nd Saloon
LIVERPOOL (Round Anglesey) -	7/6	5/-

CHILDREN OVER THREE AND UNDER TWELVE YEARS HALF FARE.

BREAKFASTS, DINNERS, AND TEAS ON BOARD OF BEST QUALITY AT MODERATE PRICES.

For further particulars apply to the Liverpool and North Wales S.S. Co., Ltd., T. G. BREW, Secretary, 40, Chapel Street, Liverpool.   Telephone No. 6366.

☞ LAST TRIP OF THE SEASON from LIVERPOOL ☞ ROUND ANGLESEY.

Note the Date: TUESDAY, September 15th.

"Guardian" General Printing Works, Manchester, Reddish, and London.

The time of the normal daily sailing from Liverpool was 10.45 am but occassionally *St. Elvies* sailed from Liverpool at 9.15 am to make a "Round Angelsey" sailing. On these trips she made no calls and arrived back in Liverpool around 8.00 pm. *[K.C. Saunders collection]*

St. Elvies in the Menai Straits with her bridge amidships and taller funnels. *[K.C. Saunders collection]*

St. Elvies, approaching Llandudno later in her career, after having had her bridge moved from midships to forward of her funnels. *[K.C. Saunders collection]*

moored off New Brighton. The *Hercules*, of the Snowdon Passenger Steamship Company, was almost cut in two and sank immediately. Her crew of nine all jumped overboard and were picked up except for the second engineer who was drowned. The bow of the *St. Elvies* was stove in and her stem twisted. Her forward compartments quickly flooded, but the water-tight bulkheads held and there was no danger of her sinking. She put alongside New Brighton pier and her passengers returned to Liverpool aboard one of the Wallasey ferries. It was established that the collision was caused by a failure of the steering gear.

Following the outbreak of the First World War the *St. Elvies* was requisitioned in March 1915 and she served as leader of 'P' Unit of the Patrol Minesweeping Service, Firth of Forth,

from 1916 to 1919. She flew the pennant of Commander L.D. Fisher, RN, whose lieutenant was William Highton RNR, a master with the Liverpool and North Wales Steamship Company.

Apart from her duties as a minesweeper, the *St. Elvies* was also a fleet tender and had the honour of carrying King George V on one occasion. As a minesweeper she gained the distinction of finding and bringing ashore, intact, the first German horned mine to come into British hands. For this extremely hazardous work Admiral Jellicoe sent the ship his personal congratulations and Lieutenant Highton was awarded the DSC.

After the war the *St. Elvies* returned to passenger service and made her first sailing on Whit Saturday in 1919 under the command of Captain Highton. Throughout the

1920s the *St. Elvies* carried out an intensive and varied programme of sailings every summer until the decision was taken to replace her. Her last voyage on Sunday 14th September 1930 was a 'Round Anglesey' excursion. The *St. Elvies* is perhaps best remembered for her Llandudno to Douglas sailings which used to be described as 'a bracing sea trip to the Isle of Man' - bracing oneself against her heaving decks and lifting one's feet up from a deck chair as the sea swilled down her flush-built promenade deck!

After her final voyage the *St. Elvies* was laid up in the Morpeth Dock, Birkenhead, and partly demolished. She was then towed on to the beach at New Ferry, and during the Spring of 1931 her hull was demolished by R. Smith and Sons.

The steam paddle tug *Columbus*, completed at Birkenhead in 1865, was owned by the Hercules Steam Co. Ltd. with William H. Dodd, of Water Street, Liverpool acting as manager. The company had a similar tug, *Hercules*, damaged in a collision with the *St. Elvies* in 1896. Mr. Dodd's family were the first owners of the *Snowdon*, launched in 1892. *[National Maritime Museum, P.911]*

St. Elvies arriving at Douglas from Llandudno. *[Roy Fenton collection]*

St. Elvies leaves the landing stage at Liverpool on her last voyage to North Wales. *[K.C. Saunders collection]*

Amalgamation with the Snowdon Passenger Steamship Company

Further tonnage came in 1899 following the amalgamation of the Snowdon Passenger Steamship Co. Ltd. with the Liverpool and North Wales Steamship Company. The Dodd family of Merseyside were tug owners who placed two of their vessels, the *Hercules* and the *Columbus*, on Sunday excursions from Liverpool to Llandudno. The accommodation was rather rough and ready, but the fare was low and the beer plentiful. Observing how the *St. Tudno* attracted a better class of passenger, W.H. Dodd persuaded the other members of the family that this was the way to run a profitable excursion business - to offer passengers a ship with comfortable accommodation built specially for the purpose. The Snowdon Passenger Steamship Company, which the Dodd family launched, went to Lairds of Birkenhead for a smart paddle steamer.

The *Snowdon* was launched in 1892 and had a certificate for 462 passengers and a speed of 14 knots. Before long she had established herself as a popular ship on the North Wales coast. On Sundays the *Snowdon* sailed from Liverpool to Menai Bridge and on weekdays from Llandudno to Caernarvon, calling at various piers on the way. Occasionally she sailed to Douglas, Blackpool or Holyhead. This

Snowdon, coming alongside with many passengers on deck. Note the furled sail forward. *[K.C. Saunders collection]*

was the general pattern of her sailings until 1899 when the Snowdon Passenger Steamship Company amalgamated with the Liverpool and North Wales Steamship Company. W.H. Dodd became managing director of the merged companies and he was the chairman from 1928 until his retirement in 1932.

In November 1915 the *Snowdon* was requisitioned and converted to a minesweeper. She was based at Harwich and her war service was uneventful. Following a refit on the Clyde in 1918, the *Snowdon* was attached to a flotilla of minesweepers based at Belfast, and it was not until 1920 that she returned to the North Wales coast, following a major overhaul.

Towards the end of her career the *Snowdon* was based at Blackpool for the 1930 summer season, taking the place of the Isle of Man Steam Packet Company's *Tynwald.* Besides making local trips in Morecambe Bay, the *Snowdon* operated excursions to Llandudno and Douglas from the Lancashire resort. At the end of the 1931 season the *Snowdon* sailed to the shipbreaking yard of Smith and Company at Port Glasgow.

Above: *Snowdon's* first class dining saloon. Below: The lounge and buffet. Both views were produced as postcards by the Pier Studio of Llandudno. *[K.C. Saunders collection]*

Top: *Snowdon* and *Bourne* (353/1908) minesweeping at Harwich on 15th April 1918. *[Imperial War Museum, Q18828]*

Middle: *Bourne* (left), formerly the *Bournemouth Queen*, with *Snowdon* alongside in 1919. *[National Maritime Museum, N.4285]*

Bottom: *Snowdon* steams along at a fair old pace after her return to the North Wales coast. *[K.C.Saunders collection]*

La Marguerite on her trials in the Clyde in 1893 wearing the colours of Palace Steamers Ltd. *[Nautical Photo Agency/K.C. Saunders collection]*

The famous *La Marguerite*

In 1904 the Liverpool and North Wales Steamship Company bought one of the finest and most popular steamers ever to sail along the North Wales coast, the famous *La Marguerite*. She had been built by Fairfield in 1894 for the service between the Thames and the continent of Palace Steamers Ltd., which operated under the management of the Victoria Steamboat Association. The ownership of the new steamer was complicated; she was actually registered with Palace Steamers from 1894 to 1895, when she reverted to Fairfield. The *La Marguerite*'s maiden voyage was from London to Boulogne

on 23rd June 1894. Marguerite was the name of one of the daughters of Arnold Williams, an energetic pioneer of improved steamboat services on the Thames.

The Victoria Steamboat Association ran into financial difficulties and in April 1895 a company known as New Palace Steamers, owned by Fairfield, was incorporated to operate the *La Marguerite*. Unfortunately the popularity of the *La Marguerite* was not sufficient to make her profitable and in 1904 Fairfield sold her to another concern in which they had a very considerable interest - the Liverpool and North Wales Steamship Company. On the North Wales coast the operating

Liverpool and North Wales Steamship Company's steamer *La Marguerite* with dark coloured paddle boxes which in later years were painted white. Note also the bands on her funnel for Palace Steamers colours and the wheel forward for her bow rudder. *[K.C. Saunders collection]*

La Marguerite landing passengers by gangways each side of the paddlebox. Note the crest in the centre of the paddle box, unfortunately partially obscured. *[K.C. Saunders collection]*

With the outbreak of war on 4th August 1914, all pleasure cruises ceased. In 1915 the *La Marguerite* was requisitioned by the Admiralty as a cross-Channel troopship, capable of carrying 1,800 men and their equipment. On 17th March of that year she left Southampton for Le Havre on her first trooping voyage, carrying the First Battalion of the 6th Regiment of the City of London Rifles. For the next four years she sailed mainly from Southampton to French ports with troops, mostly at night and without lights, a hazardous and nerve-racking dash across the Channel. She remained under the command of her regular master on the North Wales service, Captain John Young. The *La Marguerite*'s only recorded mishap came in 1917 when a boiler explosion resulted in the death of four of her firemen. By the time she was released from Admiralty service in April 1919 she had carried 360,000 troops and steamed in excess of 52,000 miles.

season was longer than on the Thames, wages somewhat lower, coal cheaper and the speed required was more modest; all good reasons for hoping for a more profitable operation.

The *La Marguerite* made a trial trip from Liverpool to Llandudno and Menai Bridge on 12th May 1904 with guests of the company on board, and berthed at the newly completed St. George's Pier at Menai Bridge. With a length of 341.6 feet, the *La Marguerite* remains to this day the longest vessel to enter the Menai Strait. At the time of this trial sailing, she still carried New Palace colours. The *La Marguerite*'s first summer season on the North Wales coast lasted from 2nd July until 12th September 1904, and her running mates were the *St. Tudno* and the *St. Elvies*. During the winter refit of 1909 to 1910 the *La Marguerite* was reboilered and given a new set of funnels which improved her appearance. Marconi wireless was installed. She occasionally sailed at Easter and during Whit Week, but her main summer season was from late June until mid-September. It is not recorded that the *La Marguerite* sailed on any route other than the principal Liverpool-Llandudno-Menai Bridge service.

After a quick refit the *La Marguerite* was chartered to the Isle of Man Steam Packet Company for the 1919 summer season. The Manx fleet had been sadly depleted as a result of the war. Huge crowds of holidaymakers flocked to the Isle of Man after the war, and the number of steamers available was quite inadequate, resulting in thousands of passengers waiting for hours in queues which at time reached a mile in length. With her funnels painted in Steam Packet colours, the *La Marguerite* became the mainstay of the Liverpool and Douglas service from late May to early September 1919. She was little altered from her pre-war days, the most noticeable change being that her bridge had been fitted with wing cabs.

The old ship was back on her regular Liverpool-Llandudno-Menai Bridge route in 1920, the first sailing being on 22nd May. By 1923 the *La Marguerite* was beginning to show signs of her age as she began her thirtieth summer of operation. A rudder chain carried away off the Great Orme at

Left: Captain Young on the bridge of *La Marguerite*. Right: Captain Young with part of the crew and the ship's mascot. *[Both: K.C. Saunders]*

La Marguerite off Bangor Pier. *[K.C. Saunders collection]*

Llandudno that year. The following year there was a breakdown of one of her paddles between Llandudno and Liverpool and the *Snowdon* had to come alongside and take off her passengers. Operating and repair costs were escalating and in 1925 the company reluctantly decided to withdraw her.

Monday 28th September 1925 had been advertised as the closing day of the season. The *La Marguerite* was bravely dressed with flags, but to many of the onlookers they seemed more like a pall as they flapped listlessly in the light airs. And so, on a dull and grey Monday morning, to the accompaniment of fireworks and much waving of handkerchiefs, the *La Marguerite* set out on her last pleasure sailing.

There was a fine farewell demonstration at Menai Bridge where the pier and pontoon were crowded with a cheering throng of people, including the local schoolchildren who had been released early to witness the departure. At Bangor little interest was displayed at the end of the *La Marguerite*'s long association with the city. More spirit was displayed at Beaumaris. Llandudno Pier was crowded with thousands of people and Captain Highton spoke a few words of acknowledgement from the bridge before the old ship sailed and turned towards Liverpool for the last time.

The *La Marguerite* was sold to T.W. Ward Ltd. for £5,000 and she left the Mersey on 22nd October 1925 for Briton Ferry in South Wales for demolition. It was estimated that during her remarkable career she had carried some 7½ million passengers and steamed about 300,000 miles.

The *La Marguerite*'s bell was presented in 1927 to the First Batallion of the 6th Regiment of the City of London Rifles in memory of them being the first troops she carried to France. During her last week of service in 1925 a deckhouse from the after end of *La Marguerite*'s promenade deck was put ashore at Llandudno where it served for many years as an office on the pier. During the reconstruction of the berthing head at Llandudno Pier in 1968 this relic of the old steamer disintegrated when attempts were made to move it using a crane.

Two second-hand paddle steamers for short cruises from Llandudno

In the decade before the First World War, the Liverpool and North Wales Steamship Company was enjoying the peak of its popularity. With the purchase of two more paddle steamers in 1907, it operated a fleet of six vessels and offered a wide range of sailings. The new additions were the *Southampton*, originally built for the Southampton, Isle of Wight and South of England Royal Mail Steam Packet Co. Ltd., and renamed *St. Elian*, and the *Rhos Trevor*, purchased from Walter Hawthorn in 1909 and renamed *St. Trillo*.

The *Southampton* was built by Barclay, Curle and Company of Glasgow in 1872, so she was already 35 years old when purchased by the North Wales company. For thirty years she had sailed on the Southampton to Isle of Wight service until sold to G. Power and Sons of Newhaven, who re-sold her to Richard R. Collard, also of Newhaven. The Liverpool and North Wales Steamship Company needed a small vessel to operate against the opposition steamers of the Colwyn Bay and Liverpool Steamship Co. Ltd., and the *St. Elian* (ex-*Southampton*) was used to attract passengers from Rhyl and Rhos-on-Sea to connect with its principal sailings. With the outbreak of war in 1914 the *St. Elian* was laid up and did not sail again - she was by now 43 years old - and was broken up in 1915.

By coincidence the *Rhos Trevor* had also been built for the Southampton company in 1876 as the *Carisbrooke*. She and her near sister, the *Prince Leopold*, were purchased by the Colwyn Bay and Liverpool Steamship Company in 1906, although the Mersey Trading Company took over as managers the following year when the *Prince Leopold* was renamed *Rhos Neigr*. On 20th July 1908 the *Rhos Neigr* foundered off Rhos-on-Sea Pier whilst on passage from Llandudno to Blackpool after striking an unidentified object. Her fifty passengers were rescued and brought ashore by boat. Some 57 years later, in April 1965, the wreck was dispersed with explosives.

Above: *St. Elian* off Rhyl Pier. *[K.C. Saunders collection]*

It should be noted that the Colwyn Bay and Liverpool Steamship Company never operated sailings direct to Colwyn Bay; although there was a pier there it was comparatively short and never had a berthing head. The pier at Rhos-on-Sea, about a mile to the west of Colwyn Bay, was used for small steamers. This pier had originally been built at Douglas, Isle of Man but in the late 1880s was dismantled and rebuilt at Rhos-on-Sea.

Following the loss of the *Rhos Neigr*, the Mersey Trading Company went out of business at the close of the 1908 season and the *Rhos Trevor* was sold to Hawthorn of Rhyl, who re-sold her to the Liverpool and North Wales Steamship Company in the spring of 1909. She was renamed *St. Trillo* and operated short coastal cruises. She had a speed of about 12 knots and a licence to carry 463 passengers.

On the outbreak of war all sailings were suspended, but by 12th August 1914 the *St. Trillo* was back in service, to be followed by the *Snowdon* on 14th August and the *St. Elvies* on 27th August. These three vessels carried on until the normal close of the season. The *St. Trillo* and the *Snowdon* carried on excursion sailings from Llandudno throughout the summer of 1915, but by 1916 the *St. Trillo* was sailing alone. Her programme of sailings continued until 29th September 1916 when she made the last ever departure by a steamer from Rhos-on-Sea pier. During a severe gale of 7th to 8th January 1917 the berthing head collapsed and was carried on to the beach at Colwyn Bay, where it broke up.

The *St. Trillo* became a minesweeper based at Liverpool from October 1916, and returned to her normal peacetime duties in 1919. Towards the end of September 1919 there was a railway strike in Britain and the *St. Trillo* was immediately pressed into service to help relieve the transport difficulties between North Wales and Liverpool. Leaving Menai Bridge at 8.00 am and calling at Bangor, Beaumaris and Llandudno, she reached Liverpool at about 1.30 pm. After loading mails, parcels and passengers she set off again, making her calls in the reverse order. This routine continued for about ten days until the strike ended.

Middle: *Rhos Neigr* lost in July 1908. *[National Maritime Museum,. A1927]*
Bottom: *Rhos Trevor* as *St. Trillo*. *[K.C. Saunders collection]*

On Thursday 14th July 1921 the *St. Trillo* struck the Swelly Rock, between the Tubular and Suspension bridges across the Menai Strait. She slid up the rock, heeled over and remained fast. Lifejackets were issued to the 290 passengers who were soon transferred to the *Snowdon* and the Blackpool pleasure steamer *Greyhound*. With the rising tide the *St. Trillo* suddenly slipped off the rock into deep water. In October 1921 the *St. Trillo* was sold to a Spanish owner who renamed her *San Telmo*.

St. Seiriol (1) - a new steamer which never sailed for the company

At the end of the 1912 season the *St. Tudno* (2) was sold to the Hamburg-Amerika Line and two years later the company intended to replace her with a new ship which would have been quite an innovation on the North Wales service. It was something of a surprise to learn that she was to be constructed by A. and J. Inglis of Glasgow, instead of by Fairfield, and that she was to be the company's first screw steamer, driven by geared turbines. The new ship was named *St. Seiriol* but due to labour problems she was not launched until 7th July 1914, just a few weeks before the outbreak of war. An unusual feature of the launching was the absence of a lady to perform the naming ceremony. Instead the chairman of the company, Henry MacIver, named the vessel.

The *St. Seiriol*'s movements following the outbreak of war are rather obscure. She ran her trials before the end of 1914, painted in her owner's colours, and afterwards was laid up at the Gareloch for a time. It is likely that the company intended to run her on the North Wales route at Easter 1915 but she was requisitioned as a transport on the cross-Channel run to France where she remained until February 1916. Following her transport duties the new *St. Seiriol* was converted to a minesweeper and on 25th April 1918 she struck a mine off Harwich and was lost with an officer and 15 crew members killed, and five wounded. The Clyde turbine steamer *Atalanta* and the North Wales company's *Snowdon* took off survivors. The *St. Seiriol* settled on the Shipwash Shoal, but she sank into the sand before any salvage operations could be effected.

Above: The Captain of *St. Seiriol* with the ship's mascot.
Below: The crew of *St. Seiriol* assembled on deck.
[Both: Imperial War Museum, Q.18837 and Q.18839]

A series of pictures from the Wallis Collection of Harwich photographs taken in the years 1915 to 1919.
Top left: *St. Seiriol* after hitting a mine off Harwich on 25th April 1918. *[Imperial War Museum, Q.102670]*
Top right: A boat goes over to the stricken ship to pick off the crew assembled on the stern. *[Imperial War Museum, Q.102669]*
Bottom left and right: Her bow breaks away and the ship sinks. *[Imperial War Museum, Q.102667 and Q.102668]*

A German minesweeper replaces the *St. Seiriol*

Following the sale of the *St. Trillo* in 1921, the Liverpool and North Wales Steamship Company replaced her with its first twin-screw steamer. She was the *Hörnum*, a vessel originally built as a minesweeper for the German Navy, but not completed until after the war. J.C. Tecklenborg of Wesermünde completed her in 1919 and she went to the Hamburg-Amerika Line as a passenger tender, and also operated on the Hamburg to Heligoland service. When purchased by the North Wales Company in 1922 her name was changed to *St. Elian* (2). She looked a smart ship on the North Wales service, even if she could not disguise her obvious 'made in Germany' appearance. By one of those strange twists of fate which occur from time to time, the *St. Elian* was the *St. Seiriol*'s replacement - she became the company's first screw steamer. Her arrival in the fleet re-opened many old sailings, and for the first time in years passengers were able to visit Bardsey Island. More frequent trips were made to Blackpool and Holyhead. In fact the *St. Elian* was a veritable maid of all work. A surviving handbill announces the *St. Elian* as taking a day excursion from Liverpool to Blackpool on Sunday 8th July 1923 at 2.45 pm, allowing one and three-quarter hours ashore, at a return fare of 4/- (20p).

In 1926 the *St. Elian* was laid up because of the coal shortage caused by the General Strike. Such supplies as the company were able to obtain later in the season were allocated to the paddle steamers *St. Elvies* and *Snowdon*. The *St. Elian* resumed her sailings in 1927, making her last run on Saturday 10th September, from Menai Bridge to Liverpool. As things turned out, this was her last sailing for the company.

The German built *St. Elian* in the Mersey. *[B.& A.Feilden/J.& M.Clarkson]*

The company's Llandudno handbill for the 1927 season, reproduced in two sections due to its extreme length, gives details of all the North Wales sailings planned to mid-August. In addition to the daily departures from Liverpool many sailings were made from Llandudno to the other Welsh resorts, around Anglesey, to Bardsey and to Liverpool. The new *St. Tudno* is featured and boat and rail connections listed. *[K.C. Saunders collection]*

In December 1927 it was announced that the *St. Elian* had been sold to the Societa Partenopea Anonima di Navigazione of Naples to operate to the islands of Capri and Ischia. She left the Mersey for Italy on 26th December. The *St. Elian* was renamed *Partenope* on her arrival in Naples in January 1928, survived the war, and her name was again changed to *Ischia* in October 1949. Following her withdrawal from passenger service the old *St. Elian* became a floating restaurant at Salerno named *Bucaniero*.

The new *St. Tudno* (2)

In 1926 the paddle steamer *La Marguerite* was replaced by a new twin-screw geared turbine steamer - the *St. Tudno* (2). Handsome and comfortable though the new *St. Tudno* was, the regular passengers did not accept her readily. Old loyalties and memories die hard.

The *St. Tudno* was launched from the Fairfield yard on 2nd February 1926 by Mrs. Margaret McMahon. On trials on 22nd April she reached 19.25 knots over the measured mile, a quarter of a knot more than her contract speed. The new ship's maiden voyage was fixed for Saturday 22nd May 1926. She received a warm send-off from Liverpool and at Llandudno rockets were fired in welcome. Owing to the difficulties of getting a screw steamer alongside, her calls at Beaumaris and Bangor were discontinued. During the 1926 season the Bangor Corporation steam ferry *Cynfal* transferred the Bangor and Beaumaris passengers from the *St. Tudno* as she proceeded towards Menai Bridge, but the arrangement was not a success and was not repeated.

The *St. Tudno* opened her first season in a difficult period when the national coal strike of 1926 seriously interfered with railway traffic and with the sailings of the company's coal-burning vessels. Being an oil burner, the *St. Tudno* continued to run, carrying large crowds and offering the public a reliable means of reaching the North Wales coast.

In 1928 the appearance of the *St. Tudno* was altered slightly by the removal of the cowl on her funnel. She remained on the Liverpool-Llandudno-Menai Bridge run, her only deviation being two sailings from Llandudno to Douglas, Isle of Man in September 1931. It is said that she undertook these two sailings because the new *St. Seiriol* (2) had been licensed only until the end of August through an error on her passenger certificate. The *St. Tudno* operated the four-day programme of Easter sailings each year from 1927 until 1931, after which the *St. Seiriol* took over.

The Admiralty requisitioned the *St. Tudno* before the outbreak of war in September 1939 and she became an examination boarding vessel. She was not a success in this role, probably because of her shallow draft (just 9 feet to allow her to navigate the Menai Strait at low water). With a head sea she behaved well, but in the most moderate of beam seas she rolled atrociously.

The Naval Movements Book for the *St. Tudno* records: 'Dover, 8th October, 1939. To be sailed to London as soon as convenient to undergo repairs. As she will probably be withdrawn from duty as a Downs ABV (armed boarding vessel), defect list is only to include items to make good damage sustained recently.'

To all intents and purposes, this was the end of the war for the *St. Tudno*. On 5th December 1939 the *St. Tudno* was transferred from service as an armed boarding vessel to use as an accommodation ship at Stangate Creek (Sheerness). Her crew was paid off on 9th December at Blackwall, and on 8th February 1940 she was towed to Sheerness. She remained there until 24th December 1944 when the Naval Movements Book records 'to return to trade'. However, the *St. Tudno* was fitted out as a depot ship for minesweepers and spent 1945 serving in this capacity on the River Scheldt before being returned to her owners in time for the 1946 summer sailings.

The *St. Tudno* (2) made her first post-war sailing from Liverpool to Llandudno and Menai Bridge on Saturday 8th June 1946. In pre-war days she had operated with first- and second-class accommodation; she re-appeared in 1946 as a one-class ship.

St. Tudno berthing at Liverpool at the commencement of her maiden voyage. *[B. & A. Feilden/J. & M. Clarkson]*

Above: Captain W. Highton DSC with Chief Officer Kearne on the bridge of the new *St. Tudno*. Captain Highton had been awarded his DSC for his service on the *St. Elvies* during the First World War. *[K.C. Saunders collection]*

Right: Views on board the *St. Tudno*.

Top to bottom:

Entrances to the lounge, tea room and ladies room. *[Author's collection]*

First class dining saloon. *[K.C. Saunders collection]*

Second class tea room. *[Bookstall - St Tudno and St. Elvies/Author's collection]*

The post-war era opened well with several good seasons. Then, slowly and relentlessly, the increase in family motoring and coach tours had its effect and the number of passengers, already reduced, grew even smaller. The *St. Tudno* was starting to show her age and on 23rd August 1959 she developed problems with her steering gear off Llandudno. Her hand-operated stern steering wheel was used for the passage back to Liverpool and she arrived almost two hours late, requiring a tug to assist her in berthing.

Sailings continued more or less normally until 1960 when troubles began to build up for the company. The season opened on 4th June but the *St. Tudno* was laid up on 9th July for the two-week duration of a seamen's strike. On 13th August

1961 the *St. Tudno* was swinging off Menai Bridge pier when she collided with, and overturned, a small yacht. Its three occupants jumped into the water when they saw that a collision was inevitable.

The *St. Seiriol* (2) was withdrawn after the 1961 season, but the *St. Tudno* opened the seasonal sailings on 9th June 1962. But as the weeks slipped by, events showed that the end was near. The financial losses following various strikes and a reduction in passenger numbers owing to a succession of dull and wet summers gave the directors no opportunity of recouping their position. The *St. Tudno* closed the 1962 season on Sunday 16th September 1962 and this proved to be her final sailing. Perhaps the most poignant moment of all was

Above: The minesweeper depot ship
HMS St. Tudno in the Medway 26th June
1942. *[Imperial War Museum, FL18527]*

Middle: *St. Tudno* arriving at Terneuzen
on the River Scheldt. *[Imperial War
Museum, A26542]*

Bottom: Minesweepers in the harbour at
Terneuzen after completing a day's work
in the River Scheldt. *St. Tudno* is the right
hand ship, J84 to the left is the Halcyon
class minesweeping sloop *HMS Franklin*.
[Imperial War Museum, A26543]

THE LIVERPOOL AND NORTH WALES STEAMSHIP COMPANY LIMITED.

DAILY SAILINGS

COMMENCING

SATURDAY, 27th MAY, to MONDAY, 25th SEPTEMBER, 1933,

"ST. TUDNO" or "ST. SEIRIOL" FROM

LLANDUDNO to MENAI BRIDGE

(WEATHER AND CIRCUMSTANCES PERMITTING).   ONE HOUR ASHORE.

P.M.

1-15

Leaves Llandudno Pier
each day at 1-15 p.m
for Menai Bridge,
due 2-30 p.m.

Steamer leaves
Menai Bridge daily at
3-45 p.m.,
due Llandudno 5-0 p.m.

The Turbine Saloon Steamer "ST. SEIRIOL"

Return Fares :

3/-

(2nd Saloon)

4/-

(1st Saloon)

BOAT and RAIL.—Affording Llandudno Passengers Long Stay at Menai Bridge

These Tickets are also issued in reverse direction.   RETURN FARE **3/9**

CHILDREN OVER 3 AND UNDER 14 YEARS HALF FARE.

ALL TICKETS ARE ISSUED, PASSENGERS AND GOODS CARRIED SUBJECT TO THE COMPANY'S CONDITIONS OF CARRIAGE,
AS EXHIBITED AT THE COMPANY'S OFFICES AND ON THE STEAMERS.

For Tickets and all further particulars apply to Steamship Booking Office, Pier Gates, Llandudno. (Tel. 7141).

17 (10)

Splendid Evening Sea Cruise

MONDAY, JULY 23rd, 1934

(Weather and circumstances permitting)

P.M.

7-30

"ST. SEIRIOL"

Will leave LLANDUDNO PIER for

A SPLENDID

P.M.

7-30

Sea Cruise to Red Wharf Bay

Due back 9-30 p.m.

2/-   Special Return Fare   **2/-**

Children over 3 and under 14 years Half Fare.

(ONE CLASS)   (ONE CLASS)

ALL TICKETS ARE ISSUED, PASSENGERS AND GOODS CARRIED SUBJECT TO THE COMPANY'S
CONDITIONS OF CARRIAGE, AS EXHIBITED AT THE COMPANY'S OFFICES AND ON THE STEAMERS.

Refreshments of first-class quality are served on board at moderate prices

All information supplied by Company's Representative: T. H. Port, Pier Gates, Llandudno (Tel. 7141).

(98)   **ALL TICKETS AT PIER GATES.**

St. Seiriol was intended mainly for the company's secondary services - excursions from Llandudno to destinations along the North Wales coast in addition to half day sailings from Liverpool to Llandudno. *[K.C. Saunders collection]*

An almost new *St. Seiriol* coming alongside the Landing Stage at Liverpool. *[M. Cooper/B. & A. Feilden/J. & M. Clarkson]*

when she was leaving Llandudno Pier for the very last time: the lanyard from the bridge to the steam whistle parted, and the old ship couldn't even say 'farewell'.

St. Seiriol (2) - a new running-mate for the St. Tudno (2)

After the entry into service of the new *St. Tudno* (2) in 1926, four years were to pass before there were any more changes to the fleet. At the close of the 1930 season the *St. Elvies* was disposed of after 35 years of service and in the following year the *Snowdon* was sold to shipbreakers.

To replace these paddle steamers the Liverpool and North Wales Steamship Company had ordered the *St. Seiriol* (2), a smaller version of the *St. Tudno* (2), from the Fairfield yard. After the *St. Tudno* had been in service for a couple of years, the difference between herself, the *St. Elvies* and the *Snowdon* became too pronounced.

At the launching ceremony on 5th March 1931, Mrs. Kenneth Lampson, daughter of the company's chairman, named the new ship *St. Seiriol*. Trials on 23rd April saw her reach 18.5 knots and a month later, on 23rd May, the *St. Seiriol* made her maiden voyage. The new ship was a smaller edition of the *St. Tudno* and her internal arrangements were essentially the same. The *St. Seiriol* would be used on the company's secondary services such as excursions from Llandudno to Douglas, half-day excursions from Liverpool to Llandudno, and she would relieve the *St. Tudno* on Fridays on the Liverpool-Llandudno-Menai Bridge run. Towards the end of her life in 1957, 1958 and 1959, the *St. Seiriol* was chartered by the Isle of Man Steam Packet Company at the peak of the summer season for a round trip from Liverpool to Douglas, leaving Liverpool at midnight on a Friday, and returning from Douglas at 8.00 am on Saturday.

The *St. Seiriol* provided a mixed programme of 'entertainment' for her passengers in her early years. On her 'Round Anglesey' sailing on Sunday 18th August 1935, attractions offered included horse racing, bingo, a balloon race, an ankle competition, a sweepstake on the time that the ship would pass South Stack, and a prize for the lucky programme number.

On Sunday 3rd September 1939 the *St. Seiriol* left Liverpool as usual for North Wales. When she was about twenty miles out, Neville Chamberlain made his fateful announcement on the radio. She went on to disembark her Llandudno passengers and then returned to Liverpool.

The *St. Seiriol* was drydocked in Herculaneum No.1 Graving Dock and shortly after the outbreak of war the Government put her to work, painted in wartime grey. She left the Mersey on 17th January 1940 for service as a troop transport across the English Channel. She served in this capacity until May 1940. After she had sailed for Cherbourg with a full complement of troops on 20th May, she was instructed to return to Dover. The *St. Seiriol* was the first ship to make for Calais two days later. Surviving heavy bombing, she arrived at the port to discover that there was no possibility of embarking troops as the Germans had taken possession. She was then ordered to leave as quickly as possible.

The *St. Seiriol* was one of the first vessels to arrive at Dunkirk at the start of Operation Dynamo. Three of her lifeboats were damaged and her wireless aerial carried away. Adjacent to the *St. Seiriol*, the well known London pleasure steamer *Crested Eagle* was embarking troops and received a direct hit from a bomb. The *St. Seiriol* went to her assistance and, working for five and a half hours in a hail of bombs, she managed to rescue about 150 burnt and half-drowned survivors from the *Crested Eagle*. The *St. Seiriol* made a total of seven crossings to Dunkirk. A few days later, on 17th June 1940, the Minister of Shipping, Ronald Cross, sent Captain Dop of the *St. Seiriol* the following message: 'I write on behalf of the Government to convey to you and the members of your ship's company the gratitude and admiration felt for the help freely given and endurance displayed by you all in the evacuation of Dunkirk. This operation, in which the Merchant Navy joined

St. Seiriol in the Clyde, acting as a tender to the troopship *West Point* (26454/1939) in June or July 1944. The *West Point* was better known as the United States Lines *America*. *[National Maritime Museum, N38145]*

as partner of the fighting services, was carried to a successful conclusion in the face of difficulties never before experienced in war. I am proud to pay tribute to your share and that of your ship's company in a great and humane adventure destined to occupy a place of honour in the pages of history.'

For some time after Dunkirk the *St. Seiriol* was laid up in the Stanley Dock at Liverpool. Then, still under the command of Captain Dop, she sailed for the Clyde and worked as a troop transport, principally to Northern Ireland.

On her release from Government service in December 1945, the *St. Seiriol* returned to her builders for reconditioning. Like the *St. Tudno*, she resumed her passenger sailings as a one-class ship. She sailed back to Birkenhead from Fairfield on 10th April 1946 and nine days later, on Good Friday, made her first post-war voyage from Liverpool to North Wales. The piers at Llandudno, Beaumaris, Bangor and Menai Bridge were crowded

with schoolchildren, most of whom had never before seen the Liverpool steamer. The Easter sailings continued to be operated by the *St. Seiriol* in 1947 and 1949, but by 1950 it was no longer economical to bring the steamer out of dock for just four days of sailings, given the vagaries of the Easter weather and falling passenger numbers.

After the 1947 season the Liverpool and North Wales Steamship Company discontinued the sailings round Anglesey. Because of silting, Caernarvon Bar was difficult to cross, even at the *St. Seiriol*'s very modest draft of eight feet nine inches, and on one of these sailings she had briefly grounded.

In the early hours of 3rd July 1958 the night watchman discovered several fires aboard the *St. Seiriol* while she lay at anchor in Llandudno Bay. The efforts of her master, Captain Alexander Kennedy, and crew members prevented a major disaster. A steward was afterwards charged with setting fire to the ship (see page 36).

Above left: Captain Kennedy on board *St. Seiriol* with Mr Davies who was retiring after fifty-one years of loyal service, Monday 19th September 1949, on the last trip of the season. *[K.C. Saunders collection]* Above right: Crew of the *St. Seiriol* on board their ship on the same day. The photo was taken by the Carbonara Company of Liverpool, a company often associated with the production of postcards. *[Carbonara Company/K.C. Saunders collection]*

St. Seiriol backs away from Douglas, Isle of Man. Note the end of Onchan Head on the left. *[V.E. Barford/Author's collection]*

The *St. Seiriol* was involved in strike action on Saturday 13th August 1960, was withdrawn from service and did not sail again that year. In 1961 the steamer completed a full season. It was still the era of prohibition of Sunday drinking in Welsh pubs and travelling on an excursion steamer was one of the few ways in which visitors to North Wales could buy a drink on a Sunday. The company decided to experiment with Sunday evening 'booze cruises' in 1961 using the *St. Seiriol* but, like the beer sold on board, they fell flat and were discontinued.

The *St. Seiriol*'s last sailing was a day excursion from Llandudno to Douglas on Wednesday 6th September 1961. After this she was laid up, as usual, in the Morpeth Branch Dock at Birkenhead for the winter months. Early in 1962 rumours were circulating that the *St. Seiriol* would not be working that year. The reasons for withdrawing the *St. Seiriol* rather than the more costly-to-run and less flexible *St. Tudno* were never stated, but it was hinted that the *St. Seiriol* needed a considerable sum spending on her before the 1962 summer. Her engines were not in such good condition, perhaps due to five years of intensive war service, whereas the *St. Tudno* had been laid up for most of the war.

On 28th February it was made known that the Isle of Man Steam Packet Company would take over the Llandudno to Douglas run with its own ships. No one felt any surprise a month later when the *St. Seiriol* was offered for sale. On 22nd October 1962 it was learnt that the *St. Seiriol* had been sold for demolition for £12,000, and on 13th November she left the Mersey for the last time. With the Dutch deep-sea tug *Ebro* ahead of her and the Mersey tug *Cedargarth* at her stern, the *St. Seiriol* left Birkenhead's Alfred Lock at 11.00 am. Her engines were silent, her decks deserted, everything battened down and her ventilators were covered in black canvas. The *St. Seiriol*'s bridge was locked and abandoned as she commenced her final trip to the breakers yard at Ghent.

A few spectators watch as *St. Seiriol* sails from Birkenhead for the very last time on 13th November 1962. The tug *Ebro*, taking her to the breakers, is on the extreme right. *[Author's collection]*

For one season only:
In the summer of 1934 the Alexandra Towing Company based the tender *Ryde* at Llandudno. The *Ryde* had been completed in 1891 by Harland and Wolff Ltd at Belfast for the Oceanic Steam Navigation Co. Ltd. as the *Magnetic* (619 tons gross).

In the early 1930s Alexandra had need of a tender for taking passengers out to liners anchored in the Sloyne and bought the *Magnetic* in 1932. After a refit she emerged in the normal Alexandra funnel colours but with a white, rather than a black, hull. Already old, *Ryde* was sold in 1935 for breaking up at Port Glasgow.

The *Lady Orme* was completed in 1888 as the *Fusilier* (251 tons gross) for David MacBrayne for services in the Oban area. In December 1934 she was bought by the Cambrian Shipping Co. Ltd. of Blackpool and in the 1935 summer season operated out of Llandudno to the Menai Strait as the *Lady Orme*. Ramsgate was her base in 1936 and then back to the North Wales coast in 1937 and now owned by the Ormes Cruising Co. Ltd. Her name was changed to *Crestawave* in 1938 and she spent most of 1938 and 1939 laid up. In October 1939 *Crestawave* was sold to Thos. W. Ward Ltd. for breaking up at Barrow. *[Both B.& A.Feilden/J. & M.Clarkson]*

P.S. "LADY ORME"

A return to short coastal cruises with a motor ship

With the entry into service of the *St. Seiriol* in 1931, the Liverpool and North Wales Steamship Company was operating just two turbine steamers. There were no short coastal cruises from Llandudno Pier, so in 1934 the Alexandra Towing Company based its tender *Ryde* at Llandudno, for one summer season only. The following year saw the return of a paddle steamer to the North Wales coast when the Cambrian Shipping Company ran the *Lady Orme* from Llandudno to the Menai Strait and on short coastal cruises. This steamer had been built at Paisley in 1888 for David MacBrayne and was well known in West Highland waters as the *Fusilier*. The *Lady Orme* was back at Llandudno for the 1937 season, and the following year appeared as the *Crestawave*, but only for a few weeks in June and July.

The Liverpool and North Wales Steamship Company responded by ordering from Fairfields a twin-screw, twin-funnel motor ship. She was launched as the *St. Silio* and was completed in time for the 1936 season. In her pre-war years the *St. Silio* was used imaginatively. She revived calls at Beaumaris and on 5th August 1936 made a unique sailing to Amlwch, a small port on the north east coast of Anglesey. At the end of the summer she was to be found offering cruises along the length of the Manchester Ship Canal.

After the war the name was changed to *St. Trillo* and she continued her somewhat routine and uninspired programme of short cruises from Llandudno Pier until the end of the 1962 season. In 1961 the *St. Trillo* emerged from winter dock with a green hull, dark green boot topping, and a white line separating the two. The change, said the company, was experimental, but if it was successful it would be applied to the *St. Tudno* and *St. Seiriol*. The idea, apparently, was to draw a comparison with Cunard's cruising 'Green Goddess', the *Caronia*. Thankfully it was not deemed successful and the senior ships never had to suffer that indignity. The *St. Trillo* returned to her original colours in time for the 1962 season.

'Little ships of summer will sail no more'

With these words the 'Liverpool Echo' announced on 19th November 1962 that a meeting of creditors had been told that the Liverpool and North Wales Steamship Company was to go into voluntary liquidation. A resolution, adopted at an extraordinary general meeting held earlier in the day, read: 'That it has been proved to the satisfaction of this meeting that the company cannot by reason of its liabilities continue its business and that it is advisable to wind up the same and accordingly that the company be wound up voluntarily'.

Passengers boarding the St. Silio at the Princes Landing Stage, Liverpool with the Isle of Man steamer Victoria *(1,641/1907) ahead of her. [B.& A.Feilden/J. & M.Clarkson]*

The company chairman, C.G. Mack, told the 'Echo': 'We have suffered a succession of summers of poor weather and it is apparent that we can no longer operate economically bearing in mind that the taste of the travelling public has changed. We must accept this, but with sadness, and Merseyside will, I know, remember with affection the little ships that sailed from her port'.

Mack reported total liabilities of £91,918, with estimated assets of £83,350 in ships and property. He told the 50 or so creditors present that they were witnessing the closing of a chapter of Liverpool's maritime history.

Apart from a succession of dull and wet summers, strike action had seriously affected sailings at the peak of the 1960 season. The *St. Tudno* was 36 years old and approaching the end of her economic life. Like a Greek tragedy the tale of woe gathered force. As a result of the *St. Tudno's* collision with a yacht off Menai Bridge pier in 1961, a writ of attachment was fixed to the foremast of the *St. Tudno* on 9th November 1962 and three days later the claimants were awarded £575 12s 6d in damages. On 25th March 1963 it was announced that the *St. Tudno* had been sold to Van Heyghens, ship breakers at Ghent, and she left the Mersey under tow for Ghent on 13th April 1963.

A scheme to save the *St. Trillo* was launched by T. Turner Pilling, managing director of the Llandudno Pier Company, and a conference was convened on 17th December 1962 to consider the possibility of buying the ship for £30,000. Pilling said he would like to see one million shilling shares offered to the public. An offer of £17,500 was made for the *St. Trillo*, but this was rejected by the liquidator.

In the event the *St. Trillo* was purchased by Townsend Brothers Ferries Ltd. on 19th February 1963 and, operated by

St. Tudno leaves Birkenhead on 13th April 1963 on her way to Ghent to be broken up. [Keith P.Lewis/Author's collection]

THE LIVERPOOL AND NORTH WALES STEAMSHIP COMPANY LIMITED

SAILINGS FROM LLANDUDNO

(Weather and other circumstances permitting)
SUBJECT TO ALTERATION WITHOUT NOTICE AND TO CONDITIONS OF CARRIAGE

COLWYN BAY CONNECTION BY TRAIN, ELECTRIC CAR or MOTOR BUS (see Bills).

Motor Vessel **"ST. SILIO"** *built 1936*

A.M. **10-45**	*DAILY Sundays included	Due back 12-30 p.m.
*SATURDAYS, also AUGUST 3, 17, 19 and 31 excepted See SPECIAL BILLS	**SEA CRUISES** Viewing **The Great Orme, Puffin Island** and the **Anglesey Coast**	FARE **2/-** ONE CLASS

P.M. **2-30**	*DAILY Sundays included **BEAUMARIS** Allowing time to visit The Castle **MENAI BRIDGE** To see the famous Suspension and Tubular Bridges	FARE **3/-** One Class Due back 6-30 p.m.
*SATURDAYS, also AUGUST 3, 17, 19 and 31 excepted See SPECIAL BILLS	Beaumaris to Menai Bridge Single **9d** Return **1/-**	

Leaves LLANDUDNO - 2-30 p.m.	*Leaves* MENAI BRIDGE 4-45 p.m.
„ Beaumaris - - 3-45 p.m.	„ Beaumaris - - - 5-15 p.m.
Arrives Menai Bridge - 4-15 p.m.	*Arrives* Llandudno - - - 6-30 p.m.

P.M. **7-45** See SPECIAL BILLS	**EVENING CRUISES** Towards PUFFIN ISLAND, ANGLESEY or LLANDUDNO BAY - COLWYN BAY	One Class **2/-** Due back 9-30 p.m.

CHILDREN OVER 3 AND UNDER 14 YEARS HALF FARE.

1st Class Coast Contracts (6 Consecutive Week-days) 18/- from any date Available on "St. Tudno," "St. Seiriol," or "St. Silio."

ALL TICKETS ARE ISSUED, PASSENGERS AND GOODS CARRIED SUBJECT TO THE COMPANY'S CONDITIONS OF CARRIAGE, AS EXHIBITED AT THE COMPANY'S OFFICES AND ON THE VESSELS.

Through Bookings for these Sailings from all principal Railway Stations at Reduced Fares, also by bus from Colwyn Bay at Crosville Motor Services, Conway Road, and Messrs. Pickfords, 22 Abergele Road, Colwyn Bay.

BUFFET AND REFRESHMENT BAR.

For all further particulars apply to the Company's Representative, T. H. Port, Pier Gates, Llandudno (Tel. 7141) ; Crosville Motor Services, Colwyn Bay (Tel. 2330) ; Messrs. Pickfords, Colwyn Bay (Tel. 2852) ; E. Stanley, Church Street, Beaumaris; H. Davies, 285a High Street, Bangor (Tel. 484) ; Crosville Motor Services Ltd., Bangor (Tel. 148) ; Menai Bridge Pier (Tel. 12) ; Messrs. Pritchard Bros., Porth-yr-Aur, Caernarvon (Tel. 219) ; L. Pritchard, Strand View, Benllech Bay ; or to The Liverpool & North Wales S.S. Co. Ltd., 40 Chapel St., Liverpool.

OFFICIAL ILLUSTRATED GUIDE (Post Free) 2d., or obtainable at Pier Gates and on Vessels

ALL TICKETS AT PIER GATES, AGENTS OR ON BOARD

12A (101)

SAILINGS FROM LLANDUDNO

(Weather and circumstances permitting   ★   Subject to alteration without notice)

s.s. St. Tudno ★ s.s. St. Seiriol ★ m.v. St. Trillo

EVERY DAY (SUNDAYS INCLUDED)
UNTIL SUNDAY, 11th SEPTEMBER
All Fares include Pier Tolls paid by the Company

		Single	Day Excursions
1-15 p.m. ST. TUDNO or ST. SEIRIOL	**MENAI BRIDGE (1 hour ashore)** Through picturesque Menai Strait. Due, 2-40 p.m. Return, 3-45 p.m. Due Llandudno, 5-0 p.m.	5/6	7/6
Sundays excepted	CIRCULAR TOUR Out by boat, return by any Crosville bus.	—	8/9 Children 4/6
Sundays included	Out by boat, return by rail (any train).	—	9/3 Children 4/8
5-15 p.m. ST. TUDNO or ST. SEIRIOL	**LIVERPOOL** Due 7-40 p.m.	12/-	Period 18/6

SUNDAYS

		Single	Day Excursions
10-45 a.m. ST. TRILLO	**MORNING CRUISE** Viewing the Great Orme and Puffin Island. Due back, 12-15 p.m.	—	4/-
2-45 p.m. ST. TRILLO	**AFTERNOON CRUISE** To Puffin Island and towards Red Wharf Bay. Due back, 4-45 p.m.	—	6/-
7-30 p.m. ST. TRILLO	**GRAND EVENING CRUISE** Towards Puffin Island. Due back 9-0 p.m.	—	4/6

MONDAYS

		Single	Day Excursions
10-45 a.m. ST. TRILLO	**MENAI BRIDGE (Isle of Anglesey)** 3½ hours ashore to visit beauty spots. Return St. Trillo 12-45 p.m. St. Tudno 3-45 p.m. Due Llandudno 2-15 p.m. 5-0 p.m.	5/6	7/6
2-45 p.m. ST. TRILLO	**AFTERNOON CRUISE** To Puffin Island and towards Red Wharf Bay. Due back, 4-45 p.m.	—	6/-
6-00 p.m. ST. TRILLO	**EVENING CIRCULAR TOUR** Through Menai Strait to Menai Bridge. Due, 8-0 p.m. Return by Crosville bus. Post Office Square 8-30, 8-47 p.m. Due Llandudno 10-20, 10-40 p.m.	5/6	7/0 Children 3/6

TUESDAYS

		Single	Day Excursions
10-15 a.m. ST. SEIRIOL 21st June to 6th Sept.	**DOUGLAS (Isle of Man)** Due, 1-40 p.m. Return, 4-30 p.m. About 2¾ hours ashore—due back, 8-0 p.m. Bus tour from Peveril Square. Tickets from the Purser, 2/-.	15/-	20/-
10-45 a.m. ST. TRILLO	**MENAI BRIDGE (Isle of Anglesey)** 3½ hours ashore to visit beauty spots. Return St. Trillo 12-45 p.m. St. Tudno 3-45 p.m. Due Llandudno 2-15 p.m. 5-00 p.m.	5/6	7/6
2-45 p.m. ST. TRILLO	**AFTERNOON CRUISE** To Puffin Island and towards Red Wharf Bay. Due back, 4-45 p.m.	—	6/-
6-00 p.m. ST. TRILLO	**EVENING CIRCULAR TOUR** Through Menai Strait to Menai Bridge. Due, 8-00 p.m. Return by Crosville bus. Post Office Square 8-30, 8-47 p.m. Due Llandudno 10-20, 10-40 p.m.	5/6	7/- Children 3/6

WEDNESDAYS
All Fares include Pier Tolls paid by the Company

		Single	Day Excursions
10-15 a.m. ST. SEIRIOL 22nd June to 7th Sept.	**DOUGLAS (Isle of Man)** Due, 1-40 p.m. Return, 4-30 p.m. About 2¾ hours ashore—due back, 8-00 p.m. Bus tour from Peveril Square. Tickets from the Purser, 2/-.	15/-	20/-
10-45 a.m. ST. TRILLO	**MORNING CRUISE** Viewing the Great Orme and Puffin Island. Due back, 12-15 p.m.	—	4/-
2-30 p.m. ST. TRILLO	**MENAI BRIDGE** A delightful cruise through Menai Strait. Due, 4-00 p.m. Return, 4-30 p.m. Due Llandudno, 6-00 p.m.	5/6	7/6
7-30 p.m. ST. TRILLO	**GRAND EVENING CRUISE** Towards Puffin Island. Due back, 9-00 p.m.	—	4/6

THURSDAYS

		Single	Day Excursions
9-30 a.m. ST. SEIRIOL 23rd June to 1st September	**LIVERPOOL (Two hours ashore)** Due, 12-00 noon. Return from Liverpool, 2-00 p.m. Due Llandudno, 4-30 p.m.	—	10/-
10-45 a.m. ST. TRILLO	**MENAI BRIDGE (Isle of Anglesey)** 3½ hours ashore to visit beauty spots. Return St. Trillo 12-45 p.m. St. Tudno 3-45 p.m. Due Llandudno 2-15 p.m. 5-00 p.m.	5/6	7/6
2-45 p.m. ST. TRILLO	**AFTERNOON CRUISE** To Puffin Island and towards Red Wharf Bay. Due back, 4-45 p.m.	—	6/-
6-00 p.m. ST. TRILLO	**EVENING CIRCULAR TOUR** Through Menai Strait to Menai Bridge. Due, 8-00 p.m. Return by Crosville bus. Post Office Square 8-30, 8-47 p.m. Due Llandudno 10-20, 10-40 p.m.	5/6	7/0 Children 3/6

FRIDAYS

		Single	Day Excursions
10-45 a.m. ST. TRILLO	**MORNING CRUISE** Viewing the Great Orme and Puffin Island. Due back, 12-15 p.m.	—	4/-
2-30 p.m. ST. TRILLO	**MENAI BRIDGE** A delightful cruise through Menai Strait. Due, 4-00 p.m. Return, 4-30 p.m. Due Llandudno, 6-00 p.m.	5/6	7/6
6-00 p.m. ST. TRILLO	**EVENING CIRCULAR TOUR** Through Menai Strait to Menai Bridge. Due, 8-0 p.m. Return by Crosville bus. Post Office Square 8-30, 8-47 p.m. Due Llandudno 10-20, 10-40 p.m.	5/6	7/- Children 3/6

Children over three and under fourteen years, half fare.
Buffets and refreshment bars on all vessels.
Lunches and teas available on St. Tudno and St. Seiriol only.
Weekly Season Tickets (not transferable) 30/- (pier tolls excluded) issued from any date and available all advertised sailings of the Company's vessels from Llandudno. Not available on bus circular tours.

FOR FURTHER INFORMATION APPLY TO;
Llandudno: Company's Representative, Pier Gates. (Tel. Llandudno 76837).
Colwyn Bay: Crosville Motor Services (Tel. 2230). Pickford's Ltd., 26 Abergele Road (Tel. 2852).
Abergele: S. A. Roberts, Amity House. Rhyl; Crosville Motor Services (Tel. 437).
Beaumaris: G. M. Evans, Medical Hall, Church Street (Tel. 39).
Bangor: Crosville Motor Services (Tel. 2448).
Menai Bridge: Pier Gates Office (Tel. 12).
Caernarvon: Pritchard Bros., Porth-yr-Aur (Tel. 219).
Conway: E. N. Cooper, Ye Corner Cafe, Lancaster Square.
Railway Stations, or the Liverpool and North Wales Steamship Co. Ltd., 40 Chapel Street, Liverpool, 3 (Tel. CENtral 1653/4).
TICKETS AT COMPANY'S OFFICE, PIER GATES, LLANDUDNO AND MENAI BRIDGE, FROM AGENCIES OR ON BOARD THE VESSELS

Opposite: A hand bill detailing cruises planned for the *St. Silio* along the coast of North Wales and Anglesey.
Above: Sailings planned for the period 4th June to 11th September 1958, weather and circumstances permitting, from Llandudno by the *St. Tudno*, *St. Seiriol* and *St. Trillo*. [Both K.C.Saunders collection]

subsidiary P. and A. Campbell Ltd., she continued to be based at Llandudno during the peak summer season until 1969 (with the exception of 1968). The *St. Trillo* was broken up on the banks of the River Liffey at Dublin in 1974.

The Liverpool and North Wales Steamship Company was wound up in 1963. The ships had all been sold and on 13th May 1963 a sale of fittings and equipment from the *St. Tudno* and *St. Seiriol* was held at a Liverpool saleroom. The contents of the office at 40 Chapel Street, Liverpool were sold on the following day. The curtain finally came down on 11th September with the disposal by auction of the office at 40 Chapel Street.

St. Trillo off Llandudno in 1961 with her *'Caronia'* green hull. For the 1962 season she reverted to her original black hull. *[Malcolm McRonald]*

Recent years

The Isle of Man Steam Packet Company took over the Llandudno and Douglas sailings after the demise of the *St. Seiriol* in 1961. From 1962 they offered two return sailings a week during the summer months. In 1963 the Manx company placed one of its steamers on the Liverpool to Llandudno service, usually three times a week during the season. The Manx steamers were too large to make the sailing to Menai Bridge, and usually anchored in Llandudno Bay during the four-hour stopover. As a result the *St. Trillo*, now operated by P. and A. Campbell Ltd., offered an increased frequency of sailings to Menai Bridge, no doubt because of the removal of the competition from the *St. Tudno*. With new owners in charge, there was at last some attempt to break the monotony of the *St. Trillo's* pattern, and sailings such as excursions to Caernarvon and, for the first time since 1947, 'round Anglesey' cruises were introduced.

In 1967 the berthing head at Llandudno Pier had deteriorated to the point whereby the Manx steamers could no longer lie alongside and so all sailings by the Manx fleet were withdrawn. The *St. Trillo* operated an extensive programme throughout the 1967 season including several Liverpool to Llandudno day excursions and frequent 'round Anglesey' sailings. Being a much smaller vessel than the Manx steamers, she was still able to berth at Llandudno and so had all the Llandudno traffic to herself with no competition.

The *St. Trillo* arrived at Llandudno on 5th May 1968 in order to act as tender to the liner *Kungsholm* the following day. There were gale force winds on 6th May and a nylon rope from the *Kungsholm* became entangled around one of the *St. Trillo's* propellers, and her other engine broke down. The *St. Trillo* anchored in Llandudno Bay and was attended by three lifeboats, but the conditions were too rough to transfer the *Kungsholm's* mainly elderly American passengers. The conditions deteriorated further, forcing the *Kungsholm* to move out to sea to a safer anchorage, whilst the *St. Trillo* was left wallowing at anchor. After several hours of this the trawler *Kilravock* towed the *St. Trillo* back to Llandudno Pier where her now desperately seasick passengers were disembarked and accommodated in local hotels. The *Kungsholm* was diverted to Liverpool to pick up her stranded passengers, and the *St. Trillo's* propeller was cleared by divers at Llandudno.

For the main 1968 summer season P. and A. Campbell needed the *St. Trillo* on the Bristol Channel to cover for the now withdrawn *Bristol Queen*. To replace her at Llandudno the *Queen of the Isles* was chartered from the Isles of Scilly Steamship Company. She was somewhat faster and certainly a better sea boat than the *St. Trillo* and managed to include a couple of Llandudno to Douglas sailings towards the end of her season.

Snaefell (2,489/1948) leaving Llandudno for Douglas in the early 1960s. Note the berthing head, lower than the main pier, in the bottom right hand corner. *[John Lawson Reay/Author's collection]*

The Manx steamers had returned to Llandudno in 1968 following the reconstruction of the berthing head at the pier. The *St. Trillo* was back at the Welsh resort on 16th May 1968 to act as tender to the *Kungsholm* the following day. She suffered yet another embarrassment in this role when strengthening winds prevented her from getting alongside on her final trip from the pier. A Welsh school folk dance party, a male voice choir and local Llandudno dignitaries were stranded on the *Kungsholm* and had to sail to the liner's next port of call, Douglas, Isle of Man, whilst a number of the cruise passengers and some of the liner's crew suffered what must have been a very sobering experience in that they had to sail on the *St. Trillo* to Douglas in the teeth of a gale in order to rejoin the *Kungsholm*.

Queen of the Isles at Liverpool. *[J.& M.Clarkson]*

The *St. Trillo* was again based at Llandudno for the 1969 season, but this was to be her swansong. She was laid up at the end of the summer in dock at Barry, South Wales, until 21st April 1974 when she made her final voyage under tow to shipbreakers at Dublin.

An occasional visitor to Llandudno between 1970 and 1975 was the former Isle of Wight ferry *Balmoral*. The main purpose of the visit was to act as tender to the visiting cruise liner *Kungsholm*, but she managed a few public sailings every year.

With the withdrawal of the *St. Trillo*, the Isle of Man Steam Packet Company operated two-hour coastal cruises from Llandudno on each day that

Balmoral in May 1974. *[J.&.M.Clarkson collection]*

the Liverpool to Llandudno sailings operated. These soon became extremely popular with over 1,500 passengers regularly on board for the sail to Point Lynas. In the mid-1970s the Llandudno to Douglas excursions operated on up to five days a week and, given good weather, each sailing attracted up to 2,000 passengers. This phenomenal success was due in no small part to the untiring enthusiasm of Gerry Bouwman, the Steam Packet Company's Llandudno agent.

With the sale of the *Mona's Isle* at the end of the 1980 summer season the Liverpool to Llandudno sailings ceased. The *Manxman* carried on a reduced Llandudno to Douglas service until she too was sold out of the Manx fleet at the end of 1982.

In 1977 the preserved Clyde paddle steamer *Waverley* visited Liverpool and carried out two Liverpool to Llandudno sailings. She was not entirely suitable for the Mersey and found it difficult to cope with the very strong tides which are encountered in the sea channels. However, the *Waverley* did return to Liverpool in June 2001 and once more visited Llandudno.

In 1982 the catamaran *Highland Seabird* attempted an ambitious programme of sailings from Liverpool to

Llandudno. Three sailings a day were advertised on Mondays, Wednesdays, Fridays and Saturdays, with one sailing on Sundays, Tuesdays and Thursdays. For a fare of £8.50 passengers could enjoy up to nine hours ashore in Llandudno. However, the *Highland Seabird* proved entirely unsuitable for the frequently encountered 'deep-sea' conditions to be found off the Mersey Bar and the venture was very quickly abandoned. Mersey Ferries also experimented with the catamaran, and quickly reached the same conclusion.

The restored *Balmoral* re-entered service in 1986 as a partner for the *Waverley*. Every year she visits the Mersey and provides some Liverpool to Llandudno sailings, occasionally proceeding to Menai Bridge and Caernarvon. The *Balmoral* has also occasionally revived the 'round Anglesey' sailing from Liverpool.

In 1997 the Isle of Man Steam Packet Company's *Lady of Mann* offered a Liverpool to Douglas excursion calling at Llandudno Pier en route. It was 15 years since a Manx vessel had last called at Llandudno, and the Llandudno to Douglas section of the sailing was a complete sell out. In recent years it has become traditional for the *Lady of Mann* to provide one or two Llandudno to Douglas excursions prior to

Lady of Mann leaving Llandudno for Douglas 22nd May 1997. *[Author]*

board the *St. Seiriol* for the night. Beds are being improvised, and the crew are making sure the passengers are all comfortable. Special attention is being paid to the welfare of children. There is plenty of food on board.'

The *St. Seiriol* left Douglas at 8.40 am the following day, 7th September, and after a rough passage arrived alongside Llandudno Pier at 12.30 pm. A large crowd on the pierhead cheered heartily as she came alongside.

1951: *St. Tudno's* Festival of Britain fireworks cruise

After arriving back at Liverpool at 7.45 pm on Friday 10th August from her regular sail to Llandudno and Menai Bridge, the *St. Tudno* embarked 2,000 passengers for a special cruise to view the firework display being held in the Mersey in conjunction with the Festival of Britain celebrations. The *St. Tudno* sailed at 8.30 pm and anchored in mid river at 8.50 pm to view the fireworks which were being set off from the Mersey's fire boat *William Gregson*. After the display the *St. Tudno* weighed anchor at 10.40 pm and was back alongside the landing stage at 11.05 pm.

1953: *St. Seiriol's* special Coronation Day afternoon cruise

Coronation Day, Tuesday 2nd June 1953, proved to be a dismal affair on Merseyside with continuous rain and a full northerly gale blowing, and the *St. Tudno's* sailings to Llandudno and Menai Bridge were cancelled because of the weather. However, the *St. Seiriol's* 'Special Afternoon Cruise' went ahead, but with a difference. She sailed from the landing stage at 2.00 pm, and proceeded down the Rock Channel. With the northerly gale still blowing it would have been impossible to berth at Llandudno, and so the *St. Seiriol* proceeded north to the Bar Lightship, giving her passengers a very rough hour. After arriving back in the Mersey the steamer sailed south to the Dingle Oil Jetty and the entrance to the Eastham Channel, before arriving back at the landing stage at 5.50 pm.

her TT Week sailings, and she has always carried a full complement of passengers. The one exception to this routine was 2001, the year of the foot-and-mouth disease outbreak. The *Lady of Mann* has now been sold out of the Manx fleet, and so 2005 proved to be her final year.

For the future it is to be hoped that the *Balmoral* will continue her annual visits to the Mersey and provide some excursions to the North Wales coast.

THE POST-WAR SUMMER SEASONS, 1946 to 1962

The last section of this book takes an in-depth look at some of the ups and downs of the Liverpool and North Wales Steamship Company during its final years based on reports in local newspapers and other sources.

1950: *St. Seiriol* stormbound at Douglas

The *St. Seiriol* left Llandudno at 10.15 am on Wednesday 6th September with 408 passengers on a day excursion sailing to Douglas and, after a choppy passage, arrived at 1.40 pm. During the afternoon a severe gale blew up and when sailing time arrived at 4.30 pm it was not thought safe for the *St. Seiriol* to leave the harbour.

Many passengers elected to spend the night on board the *St. Seiriol*, whilst others found accommodation in Douglas. The company's office at Llandudno Pier Gates displayed a notice advising that due to 'weather conditions' the ship would not leave the Isle of Man that night. Company officials remained on duty until late to deal with enquiries from anxious relatives.

Captain H. Doran (the Harbour Master at Douglas) said: 'the passengers are remaining on

St. Seiriol at Douglas on 31st August 1955. *[F.W.Hawks/K.C.Saunders collection]*

29th November 1953: sentiment saves holiday ships

It was reported that two men who love ships had saved, for sentimental reasons, the Liverpool and North Wales Steamship Company from being sold to one of the 'mystery' financial rings seeking to buy up merchant fleets. The deal would cost £250,000 and involve 400 shareholders with 63,700 shares. Behind it were Charles G. Mack, a director of the company, and Gilbert J. Innes, retired Lloyd's underwriter.

The crisis began after the company had declared a 15% dividend. A shareholder suggested that it should have been 20%. Then came two offers from financial groups of £4 each for the £1 shares - 12/6d (63p) above the highest Liverpool Stock Exchange quotation. The shareholders were eager to accept.

Charles Mack discussed the crisis with Lieutenant-Commander H. Ian MacIver, DSC, the managing director. A race against time began to save the house flag. With Gilbert Innes they formed a third take-over group. Their offer of £4 per share was accepted by the shareholders. The old management would continue running the company. 'We could not bear to think of the old flag being scrapped,' said Mack. 'My friends and I have taken over the company for sentimental reasons. All profits will be ploughed back to provide reserves for maintaining the fleet, and so the Liverpool and North Wales Steamship Company becomes a non-profit making trust.'

1954: It's a wonderful day out!

The summer of 1954 turned out to be particularly stormy. On Saturday 26th June the forward stairs from the boat deck to the shelter deck on the *St. Tudno* were washed away in a north westerly gale. A month later on 27th July the *St. Tudno* took almost five hours to reach Llandudno and on Wednesday 18th August she reached Menai Bridge, but was unable to return due to severe gales. Her passengers were returned to Merseyside by rail or bus and the *St. Tudno* returned to Liverpool the following morning. A few days later, on 24th August, the *St. Seiriol* was in a similar predicament, and on Friday 10th September she turned back to Liverpool as conditions deteriorated on passage to Llandudno.

The slogan 'It's a wonderful day out' was often used by the company to describe its sailings, and on Sunday 12th August 1954 the 'Liverpool Echo' sent a reporter and his family along to join in the fun. Here is his report:

'Not even the writer who sings Llandudno's praises in the resort's lavish guide book dared to call it the Promised Land. I will. Because to me, my wife and two-year-old son Mark, and scores of others, Llandudno became as attractive as a cool well-watered oasis in the burning desert, or as desirable as firm ground at the end of a mile-long cake walk.

'I will explain that for my trip to Llandudno I decided to go as an average tripper, taking wife, infant, thermos flask and bucket and spade for a day on and by the sea. On the sea…? Yes, we decided to go from Liverpool by boat, on the stout ship *St. Tudno*. At 10.45 we set off down the Mersey for the open sea. As we left the estuary and followed the shipping lane we noticed that the Irish Sea was pretty choppy.

'By the time we were well out the rising swell was occasionally playfully tossing fairly solid spray over the lower decks. 'It makes the trip more interesting,' I told my wife. A seasoned traveller chimed in: 'Wait until we turn along the Welsh coast and take the waves from the side. We'll roll like a drum. You'll see.'

'We did see - and feel - exactly what this gloomy know-all meant. No sooner had the course alteration been made than those standing by the weatherside rails retreated from the spray and the poor sailors on board began to look a trifle seedy.

'Soon I saw the first cardboard carton being passed around, and then heaved out to sea, well clear of the rails. I discovered, too, that it was unwise to tarry too close to the rail on the lower deck because some poor soul by the rail above had discovered that what comes up must come down! One by one passengers succumbed, and it seemed only right and proper that people who had earlier laughed at other people's upsets should later take their own turn at rail or carton, or else disappear from public view.

'My wife went below decks and stayed there so long that I asked the stewardess to go down and see if she were still among the pitiful living. My son Mark, in my arms, went yellow and then went to sleep. Every now and again a sailor would disturb our glum group and cast a sodden mop into the lively briny. After he had dangled it long enough in the foam he would pull it aboard by the attached rope and carry on mopping up. And I want to say here that the entire crew, who probably were feeling none too much like running away to sea themselves, did all they could to help us. But nothing, nothing in this wide world, would have been so welcome as the firm deck of Llandudno Pier. Soon we could see it coming, like a ray of hope at an undertakers' convention.

'Then we were very near.

'Then we were past it and heaving our way across Conway Bay. A red flag at the pier head signalled 'Do not land' - too windy we presumed - and sent us packing to Menai Bridge. Paradise Postponed!

'As the news went round, hardy types who had clung to their dignity gave in and made for the rail. And one young man who added sound effects set off a chain reaction. I might have been an average tripper, but this trip was far from average.

'Centuries later, it seemed, we entered soothing calm water and finally reached Menai Bridge. Here we entrusted ourselves to a bus which took us to Llandudno - the Promised Land.'

Checking the log for the St. Tudno on that stormy day, 1,200 passengers left Liverpool. Only 700 returned from Menai Bridge. Presumably the remaining 500 elected to return by bus or train! JS.

1955: 'For the love of Mike…'

After the storms of 1954 there was plenty of fine, sunny weather around in 1955. It was a good summer for the company with capacity loads being carried on some days, especially weekends in late July and early August. The *St. Tudno* had a passenger certificate for 2,493 and the *St. Seiriol* 1,556. The season got off to a good start on Whit Monday, 30th May, when the *St. Tudno* sailed from Liverpool at 10.45 am with 2,200 passengers. The *St. Seiriol* followed her on the afternoon cruise at 2.00 pm with a full load of 1,500 passengers. On Tuesday 26th July over 300 intending passengers were turned away from the *St. Tudno* as she had her full complement on board leaving Liverpool.

The purser of the *St. Tudno* was Edwin B. Hindley of Wallasey. He was very well known to the regulars and one of his jobs was to make the routine announcements over the

Tannoy system advising passengers about the ship's arrival times at Llandudno Pier. Hindley was also very concerned about children climbing on the ship's rails and about passengers feeding the ever present flocks of seagulls which accompanied the *St. Tudno*. These well-fed gulls regularly dive-bombed the passengers with messy results. On one particularly busy day, recalls Malcolm McRonald, a harassed Hindley completed his routine announcements with the unforgettable words 'For the love of Mike, don't feed the seagulls!'

Disobeying Purser Hindley by feeding the gulls on a North Wales steamer. *[Tierney/K.C.Saunders collection]*

1956: more storms, opposition and dead low water

After a good season in 1955, the following year produced the worst weather of the post-war seasons. Gale followed gale with sailings cancelled or aborted. It became a lottery as to whether passengers could be landed at Llandudno Pier - day after day the *St. Tudno* had to miss the call at the pier and proceed direct to Menai Bridge. Passenger numbers were very low. On Monday 3rd September the company decided that enough was enough, and the *St. Tudno* went into winter dock, leaving the smaller *St. Seiriol* to carry on until the advertised end of the sailings on Monday 17th September.

For the first time since 1937, the company experienced some competition in the form of the ex-Fairmile B motor-launch *Cambrian Prince*, a vessel built for the Royal Navy in 1941. A company styling itself Cambrian Marine Ltd. was formed and the *Cambrian Prince* was scheduled to make three non-landing cruises from Llandudno Pier every day throughout the summer. Her master was Captain R.M. Shaw who remarked 'She is a good sea boat, even if she is a little lively.' However, the gales of the 1956 summer were just too much for the *Cambrian Prince* and she was withdrawn at the end of the season.

On Tuesday 4th September the *St. Seiriol* was approaching Llandudno Pier on her way back from Menai Bridge when it was noticed that there was very little water alongside the berthing head. It was dead low water on a spring tide, and even with her draft of just eight feet and nine inches, the *St. Seiriol* could not safely approach the pier. Accordingly she anchored in the bay, and the *St. Trillo* was pressed into service to act as tender to embark the Liverpool-bound passengers. A company representative

said 'This has never happened before. The passengers had their usual time ashore, and there was no difficulty in getting them aboard.' The *St. Seiriol* left Llandudno 50 minutes late.

1958: arson attack on the *St. Seiriol*

The *St. Seiriol* arrived back at Llandudno from her day excursion to Douglas at about 8.00 pm on Thursday 3rd July. After discharging her passengers she moved to an overnight anchorage in Llandudno Bay. At about 3.00 am the following morning the ship's night watchman smelt burning and roused the master, Captain A. Kennedy. They found that the bilge had been spattered with oil and was ablaze. Two other small fires, in the dining saloon and the bar, were dealt with by the crew.

The *St. Seiriol* sailed light to Liverpool early on Friday morning, 4th July in order to take the day's sailing to Llandudno and Menai Bridge. C.I.D. officers met her on arrival and the entire crew, totalling almost 75, gave statements and were finger printed. Thomas Thompson, aged 25, a steward on *St. Seiriol*, made a signed confession, saying that he had been 'given the sack' and that he wanted to get his own back on the chief steward. Judge Laski told Thompson at Liverpool Crown Court that his offence might have had disastrous consequences and sentenced him to two years' imprisonment.

1959: a fine, sunny summer, but a lot of fog

The *St. Seiriol* opened the season on Saturday 16th May in brilliant, early summer weather. There was a good loading with 900 passengers on board and this improved to 1,200 the following day, Whit Sunday. On Bank Holiday, Whit Monday, 18th May there were angry scenes on the landing stage as over 300 intending passengers were turned away from the ship as she was carrying a full complement. Company secretary H.V. Williams apologised to them, but added, somewhat unhelpfully 'You should have been here earlier'. Many of the 300 unlucky passengers dashed along the landing stage and joined the Isle of Man steamer *Snaefell* for a day sail to Douglas.

Although fair weather predominated throughout the summer of 1959 there was a lot of fog around and on Wednesday 27th May the *St. Tudno* left Liverpool for Llandudno and Menai Bridge with a good loading of 1,200 passengers. The day was hot and hazy, but on the run back to Liverpool visibility closed down and the *St. Tudno* was forced to anchor about 300 yards off the Q1 buoy near the Bar

Cambrian Prince berthed on Llandudno Pier. *[J. & M. Clarkson collection]*

Lightship in thick fog at 6.45 pm. She lay at anchor until 10.30 pm when she entered the sea channels. Further fog banks were encountered but the *St. Tudno* proceeded slowly and arrived at the landing stage at 12.45 am, some five hours late.

One of the first passengers ashore was a Miss Flora Williams of Manchester who told the 'Liverpool Daily Post' 'It was a thrilling experience. Whilst we were at anchor various parties joined in community singing and no one appeared to be a bit worried. The only thing that did concern us was the arrangements for getting home. Everything had been arranged by the company, however, and it is good to know that we shall not have to spend the night sleeping on the landing stage. No one went hungry in the long delay as there was plenty of food on board.'

Members of the crew moved among the passengers and reassured them that everything would be all right. One passenger commented 'After the heat of the day at Llandudno it was terribly cold, and we all crowded below for warmth. Everyone was cheerful despite the great inconvenience.' Outside the radio officer's cabin there was a long queue of passengers anxious to inform relatives of the delay. The queue was so long at one time that passengers were advised not to wait as if all the messages were accepted, they could not be transmitted before midnight.

Liverpool police and the offices of the company were inundated with telephone calls from people in all parts of Lancashire inquiring about relatives who were on board the *St. Tudno*. The master, Captain R. Dop, told the 'Daily Post': 'Everybody on board was happy despite the delay. They sang to keep themselves cheerful and luckily the beer held out!'

British Railways' emergency plans to get the passengers home included a steam train standing by to go anywhere within reason, a diesel train standing by to go to Manchester, and the Southport, Ormskirk and Wirral lines remaining open.

Presentation to Captain Dop, on his retirement, from the contract holders. *[Author's collection]*

1960: more stormy weather, industrial action, 'man overboard' and Captain Dop's retirement

The season got off to a good start at Whitsun. The *St. Tudno* was in service to avoid a repetition of Whit Monday 1959 when the *St. Seiriol* had to turn away passengers. On Bank Holiday, Monday 6th June, the *St. Tudno* carried a nearly full complement of 2,200 passengers on the Llandudno and Menai Bridge run.

After that it was all down hill. Just two days later a full southerly gale prevented the *St. Tudno* from entering the Menai Strait and at a point off Puffin Island she turned back to Llandudno. Four days after this, on Sunday 12th June, the *St. Tudno* reached a point off the Little Orme at 1.20 pm on the run to Llandudno and Captain Dop thought it advisable to return to Liverpool as a south-westerly gale made it impossible for his ship to berth at Llandudno or enter the Menai Strait. And so it went on.

On Saturday 18th June a passenger jumped overboard from the *St. Seiriol*. The steamer was approaching Llandudno on the afternoon sailing from Liverpool when Raymond Pemberton, a 21 year-old bus conductor from Bradford, took the plunge. The *St. Seiriol* lowered a boat and Pemberton was quickly picked up and on the ship's arrival at Llandudno was taken to hospital. Captain Kennedy of the *St. Seiriol* said that it was the first time in his experience that he had lost a passenger overboard. The rescue operation, in charge of Second Officer Robert Jones of Amlwch, took just eight minutes. Pemberton quickly recovered in hospital and was returned to the *St. Seiriol* for passage back to Liverpool. He spent the return journey wrapped in a blanket in a cabin whilst his clothes were dried in the engine room!

On Saturday 9th July the *St. Seiriol*'s sailings were cancelled due to a seamen's strike. On the following day the *St. Tudno* was also cancelled. Both steamers were taken into dock on Tuesday 12th July and remained there until Friday 22nd July when sailings resumed. The Isle of Man steamers and the *St. Trillo* at Llandudno were unaffected. On Saturday 13th August renewed industrial action affected the *St. Seiriol* and three days later she was taken into winter dock. The company had had enough; it was a poor season and this was the last straw. The *St. Tudno* sailed on until the advertised end of the season on Sunday 11th September.

Captain Robert Dop of the *St. Tudno*, one of the best loved shipmasters on the Mersey, retired on Sunday 11th September and was given a very emotional farewell from the passengers. The contractors had clubbed together and raised £22 to buy him a gift. Captain Dop had been born at Port Dinorwic, Caernarvon in 1895 and went to sea in 1910 at the age of 15, starting his career in the old Welsh schooners in the coasting and near-continental trades. In his own words, he 'came up through the hawse pipe', the hard way. He spent time with the Leyland Line on the North Atlantic, and on the Holyhead and Dublin steamers of the London and North Western Railway.

Captain Dop gained his master's certificate in 1919 and joined the Liverpool and North Wales Steamship Company in 1920 as second officer of the *St. Elvies*. He was promoted to chief officer the following year and remained with the *St. Elvies* until she made her last voyage to Port Glasgow to be broken up in 1930. His next appointment was as chief officer of the new *St. Seiriol*, and he became her master in 1933.

Under the command of Captain Dop, the *St. Seiriol* became the first ship to reach Dunkirk on 26th May 1940. The ship was continually bombed and machine-gunned, and some damage and casualties were sustained, but time and again Captain Dop brought the *St. Seiriol* back to Dover, fully laden with troops. The remainder of the war was less adventurous for Captain Dop and the *St. Seiriol*. He was still master of the *St. Seiriol* when she re-opened the North Wales sailings on 19th April 1946 and remained with her until he transferred to the *St. Tudno* in 1949. After retiring from the Liverpool and North Wales Steamship Company in 1960, Captain Dop was appointed Piermaster at Llandudno in 1964, a position he held until 1968, when he retired owing to ill health.

1961 and 1962: like a Greek tragedy, the tale of woe gathered force

The *St. Seiriol* opened the 1961 summer season's sailings on Saturday 20th May and the *St. Tudno* came out of winter dock on 17th June under the command of Captain Pritchard. The weather was poor and the passenger numbers even poorer. On Sunday 16th July 1961 the *St. Tudno* left Liverpool with just 210 passengers; 73 disembarked at Llandudno and a mere 30 joined for the sail to Menai Bridge. Leaving Llandudno on the same day, the *St. Seiriol* had only 70 passengers on board for the 6.30 pm departure to Liverpool. This was the height of the season and it was obvious that this state of affairs could not continue. On Sunday 13th August the *St. Tudno* came into contact with a yacht whilst she was manoeuvring at Menai Bridge and caused extensive damage. After returning to Llandudno from Douglas on Wednesday 4th September the *St. Seiriol* went into winter dock at Birkenhead. She was never to sail for the company again.

In 1962 the *St. Tudno* sailed alone on the principal service to Llandudno and Menai Bridge. Cancelled sailings due to adverse weather were again frequent - on 24th June,

Captain Pritchard, Master of the *St. Tudno* in 1961 and 1962. *[Author's collection]*

26th August and 12th September. A court case was pending over the incident with the yacht the previous summer and heavy damages were expected to be awarded against the *St. Tudno*.

What turned out to be the final sailing took place on Sunday 16th September. The *St. Tudno* sailed at 10.45 am in typical mid-September conditions: a strong north-westerly breeze and a rough sea. She arrived at Llandudno on time at 1.15 pm, and was alongside at Menai Bridge at 2.45pm. The 'galley telegraph' was rife with rumour - which sadly turned out to be true - the *St. Tudno* would be following in the wake of the *St. Seiriol* to shipbreakers at Ghent. The old ship left Llandudno Pier for the final time at 5.15 pm and as Captain Pritchard reached for the whistle lanyard to blow farewell blasts, it snapped. The *St. Tudno* couldn't even say 'farewell' to the crowds on the pier and in complete silence she swung in Llandudno Bay and set course for Liverpool. It was all over.

With a scattering of snow on her decks, a forlorn *St. Tudno* lies in Morpeth Dock, Birkenhead in January 1963, awaiting her final orders. *[Author's collection]*

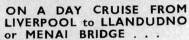 # It's a wonderful Day out

 ## First Class CATERING

ON A DAY CRUISE FROM LIVERPOOL to LLANDUDNO or MENAI BRIDGE . . .

A cruise on the "St. Tudno" or "St. Seiriol" makes the ideal outing for large or small parties. Without a care in the world you can do just as you please . . idle away happy hours on the promenade and boat decks, in the comfort of a deck chair . . . or perhaps take a drink with your friends . . you'll really relax and you'll thoroughly enjoy every minute

Catering on "St. Tudno" and "St. Seiriol" is of a particularly high standard and excellent meals are served. The dining saloons, cafeteria, refreshment bars and lounges are equipped on up-to-date lines and decorated in pleasing style.

Special reservations are made in the dining saloon for parties requiring meals. There are also buffets and a cafeteria on board for passengers requiring light refreshments only.

 ALL VESSELS FULLY LICENSED

Some of the Sights you see

The coast and mountain scenery of North Wales is always in sight on a clear day. You can see the coast resorts from Prestatyn to Colwyn Bay and watch out for the Little Orme and its monster brother the Great Orme standing sentinel over the beautifully curved Llandudno Bay. The sail down the enchanting Menai Strait will appeal to you. All this and 4 hours ashore at Llandudno or 1 hour at Menai will make it an outing you'll long remember.

Lots to do Aboard

There's something for everyone . . Music relayed by loudspeakers . . . Deck chairs for those who want to take it easy . . . . Splendid covered accommodation for all . . Excellent dining and refreshment facilities, modern self-service Cafeterias and Tuck shop for the children . . . . also bars for those who like a drink.

SPECIMEN MENUS

LUNCHEONS 8/-	TEAS 7/-
Children 5/6	*Children 4/6*
Soup	Fried Fish
Grilled Fish Fillets—Lemon	Chipped or Saute Potatoes
or	or
Roast Joint	Kippered Herrings
Vegetable	or
Boiled and Baked Potatoes	Cold Roast Joint
	Salad in Season
Fruit and Ice Cream	Tea, Bread and Butter
or	
Biscuits and Cheese	Preserves
	Cold Chicken and Ham 1/- extra
Roast Chicken 1/- extra	Cakes and Pastries served at extra charges.

Special menus can be quoted if required.

REDUCED FARES
available for
ALL PARTIES, WORKS OUTINGS, ETC., ETC.
from 24th May to 11th September

	Number of Passengers				
	Day Return		*and*	Single Journey	
	8–50	51–150	151 *over*	8–50	51–150
Liverpool & Llandudno	13/6	13/-	12/6	9/6	9/-
Liverpool & Menai Bridge	16/-	15/6	15/-	11/6	11/-
Liverpool & Llandudno—					
Half-Day Excursion 2 p.m.	8/6	*Return*			

Children over 3 and under 14 years—Half Fare

One promoter's pass allowed for parties numbering 25 passengers with an additional pass for every 50 passengers in excess of this number. Car Park facilities are available five minutes away from the Princes Stage

LLANDUDNO TO MENAI BRIDGE

If your day's outing is to Llandudno by coach or rail, why not have a cruise through the Menai Strait to Menai Bridge, with one hour ashore to see the famous Suspension Bridge. The Steamer leaves Llandudno at 1.15 p.m., due Menai Bridge 2.40 p.m. Leaving Menai Bridge 3.45 p.m. Due Llandudno about 5.00 p.m.

FARES: 6/- Return — 4/6 Single Journey

Souvenir Guide 1/-

Section of Dining Saloon.

4 hours ashore in Llandudno or one hour at Menai Bridge

The hand bill for the 1958 season. The only sailings listed are those between Liverpool, Llandudno and Menai. The remainder gives details of what to do on board, catering and a sample menu. Little to offer in comparison with hand bills of the 1920s and 1930s. *[K.C. Saunders collection]*

FLEET LIST

Notes on the ships' histories

On the second line is given the ship's official number (O.N.) in the British Register; then her tonnages at acquisition, gross (g), net (n), followed by dimensions: overall length x breadth x draft in feet.

The third line gives the number of passengers, if known, and any call sign allocated. On the fourth line is a description of the engines fitted and the name of their builder plus the horsepower and ship's speed, if known.

Subsequent lines give the details of builder and the ship's full career, including dates when registered and when the its last UK registration was closed. Dates are given to the exact day when known; for sales these are the dates of the bill of sale, for renamings the date when the new name was registered. The port listed after the title of the owning company is where the owners are based.

Details are taken from the Closed Registers in class BT110 in the National Archives, the Liverpool Registers in the Merseyside Maritime Museum, and Lloyd's Register of Shipping.

1. ST. TUDNO (1) 1891-1912 Steel paddle steamer
O.N. 97861 794g 96n 265.4 x 32.6 x 11.4 feet.
Passengers: 1,061.
C. 2-cyl. by the Fairfield Shipbuilding and Engineering Co. Ltd., Govan; 725 NHP, 3,850 IHP, 18.5 knots (20.4 knots on trials).
9.4.1891: Launched by the Fairfield Shipbuilding and Engineering Co. Ltd., Govan (Yard No. 360).

13.5.1891: Registered in the ownership of the Liverpool and North Wales Steamship Co. Ltd., Liverpool as ST. TUDNO.
6.1891: Completed at a cost of £50,000.
17.9.1912: Sold to Thomas W. Tamplin, London.
1.10.1912: Sold to the MacIver Steamship Co. Ltd., Liverpool (Thomas W. Tamplin, London, manager) for £19,000 on behalf of Hamburg-Amerika Linie, Hamburg and chartered by the Hamburg-Amerika Linie

for £330 per month for use as a tender at Southampton.
21.9.1914: Requisitioned by the Admiralty.
1918: Condemned as a prize by the High Court, as Germans were deemed to be in control of the owning company.
1921: Sold by the Admiralty Marshall to T.C. Pas, Holland.
5.1922: Broken up in Holland.
13.11.1922: Register closed.

Opposite: *St. Tudno* on trials in the Clyde Estuary. *[Glasgow University Archives DC101/0550 (X1) and (X2)]*

Above: *St. Tudno* at sea. *[K.C. Saunders collection]*

Middle and bottom: *St. Tudno* in the White Star Dock, later known as Ocean Dock at Southampton after her sale. The stern view is dated 15th September 1913.
[Middle: Nautical Photo Agency/K.C. Saunders collection, bottom F.W. Hawks, 12907]

2. BONNIE PRINCESS 1891-1896 Iron paddle steamer

O.N. 86194 434g 92n 240.0 x 26.2 x 9.3 feet.

Diagonal oscillating engines by A. Campbell and Son, Glasgow; 160 NHP, 14 knots.

Passengers: 620.

1882: Launched by T.B. Seath and Co., Rutherglen (Yard No. 215).

11.6.1882: Registered in the ownership of the Liverpool, Llandudno and Welsh Coast Steamboat Co. Ltd., Liverpool as BONNIE PRINCESS.

11.3.1891: Sold to Richard Barnwell, Govan.

15.5.1891: Acquired by the Liverpool and North Wales Steamship Co. Ltd., Liverpool.

9.5.1896: Sold to James Power, London.

8.8.1896: Sold to the Hastings, St. Leonards and Eastbourne Steamboat Co. Ltd., Hastings.

13.9.1898: Sold to Thomas W. Ward, Sheffield.

12.10.1899: Register closed on sale to Holland.

1899: Broken up by T.C. Pas, Holland.

Bonnie Princess. [Gwynedd Archives]

3. ST. ELVIES 1896-1931 Steel paddle steamer

O.N.105390 567g 149n 240.6 x 28.3 x 10.2 feet

Passengers 991. Call sign: JGCS.

C.2-cyl. by the Fairfield Shipbuilding and Engineering Co. Ltd., Govan; 450 NHP, 2,750 IHP, 19 knots (trials), 18 knots (service).

13.4.1896: Launched by the Fairfield Shipbuilding and Engineering Co. Ltd., Govan (Yard No. 391).

14.5.1896: Registered in the ownership of the Liverpool and North Wales Steamship Co. Ltd., Liverpool as ST. ELVIES.

14.9.1930: Last voyage.

1931: Sold to R. Smith and Sons. Partly demolished in Morpeth Dock, Birkenhead; hull broken up on New Ferry beach.

13.4.1932: Register closed.

St. Elvies in the Menai Straits. [B.A.Feilden/J.& M.Clarkson]

4. SNOWDON 1899-1931 Steel paddle steamer

O.N. 99404 338g 134n 167.9 x 24.6 x 10.7 feet
Call sign: JGCQ.
C. 2-cyl. by Laird Brothers, Birkenhead; 200 NHP, 1,000 IHP, 14 knots.
26.4.1892: Launched by Laird Brothers, Birkenhead (Yard No. 588).
21.5.1892: Registered in the ownership of the Snowdon Passenger Steamship Co. Ltd., Liverpool as SNOWDON.
4.5.1899: Acquired by the Liverpool and North Wales Steamship Co. Ltd., Liverpool.
1931: Broken up by Smith and Company at Port Glasgow at end of the season.
21.3.1932: Register closed.

Top: *Snowdon.* [K.C. Saunders collection]

Middle: *Snowdon* off Bangor. The small coaster behind her bow is the *Solway Firth*. In the left background is the *Clio*. Completed in 1858 as a wooden screw corvette she became a training ship in 1876. Sold out of the Royal Navy in 1919 she was broken up at Bangor. [K.C. Saunders collection]

Bottom: *Snowdon* later in her career. The steadying sail apparent above is no longer visible and the funnels appear to be taller, less raked and painted in only one shade. [World Ship Society Limited]

5. LA MARGUERITE 1904-1925 Steel paddle steamer
O.N. 102875 2,205g 1,092n 341.6 (330.0) x 40.0 x 21.6 feet.
Call sign: NKHT.
Two C.2-cyl. by the Fairfield Shipbuilding and Engineering Co. Ltd., Govan; 1,200 NHP, 8,000 IHP, 21 knots (trials), 21.5 knots (register).

1894: Launched by the Fairfield Shipbuilding and Engineering Co. Ltd., Govan (Yard No. 375).
15.6.1894: Registered in the ownership of the Palace Steamers Ltd. (Victoria Steamboat Association, managers), London as LA MARGUERITE.
30.4.1895: Sold to the Fairfield Ship-building and Engineering Co. Ltd., London.

26.3.1904: Acquired by the Liverpool and North Wales Steamship Co. Ltd., Liverpool.
1925: Sold to T.W. Ward Ltd. for demolition at Briton Ferry.
22.10.1925: Sailed from the Mersey for South Wales.
19.6.1926: Register closed.

La Marguerite in the Mersey. *[B.& A. Feilden/J. & M. Clarkson collection]*

The marvellous *La Marguerite*.

Top: Coming alongside at Llandudno.

Middle left: "All aboard", everyone seems to be standing around awaiting departure. The ship's builders plate is prominent just below the canvas dodger of the bridge.

Middle right: Under way and smoking well.

Bottom: At her winter berth in Morpeth Dock, Birkenhead. The Mersey Docks and Harbour Company's dredger *Leviathan* is in the background and a Mersey ferry ahead of her. *[All K.C. Saunders collection]*

6. ST. ELIAN (1) 1907-1915 Iron paddle steamer

O.N. 62236 203g 83n 150.1 x 20.1 x 8.7 feet.

Compound diagonal engines by Barclay, Curle and Co., Glasgow; 84 ENHP, 11 knots.

1872: Completed by Barclay, Curle and Co., Glasgow (Yard No. 230).

9.8.1872: Registered in the ownership of the Southampton, Isle of Wight and South of England Royal Mail Steam Packet Company Ltd., Southampton as SOUTHAMPTON.

7.1.1901: Sold to James Power, London.

11.10.1902: Sold to Richard R. Collard, Newhaven.

9.10.1907: Renamed ST. ELIAN.

20.7.1907: Acquired by the Liverpool and North Wales Steamship Co. Ltd., Liverpool.

1914: Laid up on outbreak of First World War and subsequently broken up at Briton Ferry.

15.4.1915: Register closed.

7. ST. TRILLO (1) 1909-1921 Iron paddle steamer

O.N. 72360 164g 89n 165.7 x 20.1 x 8.0 feet.

Compound diagonal engines by Barclay, Curle and Co., Glasgow; 70 NHP, 12 knots.

Passengers: 463. Call sign: JGCR.

1876: Completed by Barclay, Curle and Co., Glasgow (Yard No. 260).

29.3.1876: Registered in the ownership of the Southampton, Isle of Wight and South of England Royal Mail Steam Packet Co. Ltd., Southampton as CARISBROOKE.

9.11.1905: Sold to Richard R. Collard, Newhaven.

23.11.1905: Sold to William Horton, Colwyn Bay.

5.5.1906: Sold to the Mersey Trading Co. Ltd. (Alexander W. Watt, manager) Liverpool.

23.5.1907: Renamed RHOS TREVOR.

1.6.1908: Sold to Walter Hawthorn, Rhyl.

15.4.1909: Acquired by the Liverpool and North Wales Steamship Co. Ltd., Liverpool.

4.5.1909: Renamed ST. TRILLO.

28.10.1921: Register closed on sale to Marques de Olaso, Bilbao, Spain and renamed SAN TELMO.

1930: Sold to Linea de Vapores Sevilla-Sanlucar, Seville, Spain.

1935: Broken up.

8. ST. SEIRIOL (1) 1914-1918 Twin-screw geared turbine steamer

O.N. 137413 928g 402n 239.6 x 30.1 x 10.5 feet.

Call sign: JHGD.

Rotary engines by A. and J. Inglis Ltd., Pointhouse, Glasgow; 17 knots.

9.7.1914: Launched by A. and J. Inglis Ltd., Pointhouse, Glasgow.

Top: *Southampton* in the ownership of Richard R. Collard later became the company s first *St. Elian*. [*Ambrose Greenway collection*]
Middle: *St. Elian* sailed for the company for only seven years before being laid up and sold for breaking. [*Carbonara Company/K.C.Saunders collection*]
Bottom: *St. Trillo* was owned by the company for twelve years before being sold for further service in Spain. [*K.C. Saunders collection*]

10.11.1914: Registered in the ownership of the Liverpool and North Wales Steamship Co. Ltd., Liverpool as ST. SEIRIOL.
1915: Requisitioned as a troop transport and later became a minesweeper.
25.4.1918: Struck mine off Harwich and sank.
24.5.1918: Register closed.

9. ST. ELIAN (2) 1922-1927 Steel twin-screw steamer

O.N. 145954 505g 193n 186.4 x 24.0 x 10.7 feet.
Passengers: 528. Call sign: KMHQ.
Two T.3-cyl. by J.C. Tecklenborg A.G., Wesermünde; 318 NHP, 1,240 IHP, 14.5 knots.
1919: Completed by J.C. Tecklenborg A.G., Wesermünde as a minesweeper for the Imperial German Navy.
1919: Purchased by Hamburg-Amerika Paketfart A.G., Hamburg, Germany and renamed HÖRNUM.
19.6.1922: Registered in the ownership of the Liverpool and North Wales Steamship Co. Ltd., Liverpool as ST. ELIAN.
5.11.1927: Register closed on sale to Societa Partenopea Anonima di Navigazione, Naples, Italy and renamed PARTENOPE for the Naples to Capri and Ischia services.
10.1949: Renamed ISCHIA
1972: Deleted from Lloyd's Register. Converted to floating restaurant and renamed BUCANIERO, based at Salerno until at least 1991.

The only known photograph of the *St. Seiriol*. The Liverpool and North Wales photographers never had a chance to see her. This photograph has been retouched considerably but is probably a good likeness of her. *[K.C.Saunders collection]*

Middle: *St. Elian* under Italian ownership as the *Ischia*. *[Ambrose Greenway collection]*
Bottom: *St. Elian* coming alongside at Liverpool. *[B.& A. Feilden/J. & M. Clarkson collection]*

10. ST. TUDNO (2) 1926-1963 Steel twin-screw steamer

O.N. 147367 2,326g 943n 318.4 x 44.1 x 20.5 feet.

Passengers: 2,493. Call sign: GMPQ.

Four steam turbines, single reduction geared to two screw shafts by Fairfield Shipbuilding and Engineering Co. Ltd., Govan; 742 NHP, 4,100 BHP, 19 knots.

2.2.1926: Launched by the Fairfield Shipbuilding and Engineering Co. Ltd., Govan (Yard No. 618).

30.4.1926: Registered in the ownership of the Liverpool and North Wales Steamship Co. Ltd., Liverpool as ST. TUDNO.

16.9.1962: Final voyage

28.3.1963: Register closed on sale to Belgium.

13.4.1963: Left Mersey under tow of NORDZEE having been sold to Van Heyghen Frères S.A., Ghent for breaking up.

5.1963: Demolition began.

Top: The almost complete *St. Tudno* at the fitting-out berth in Fairfield's yard on the Clyde. *[J. & M. Clarkson collection]*

Middle: In the Mersey flying her pennant at the foremast and the company flag at her main. *[B. & A. Feilden/J. & M. Clarkson collection]*

Bottom: Off Llandudno with the company houseflag clear for all to see. *[Author's collection]*

48

11. ST. SEIRIOL (2) 1931-1962 Steel twin-screw steamer

O.N.162343 1,586g 657n 269.7 x 37.1 x 19.4 feet

Passengers: 1,560. Call sign: GPCR.
Four steam turbines, single-reduction geared to two screw shafts by Fairfield Shipbuilding and Engineering Co. Ltd., Govan; 596 NHP, 3,300 BHP, 18$\frac{1}{2}$ knots.

5.3.1931: Launched by the Fairfield Shipbuilding and Engineering Co. Ltd., Govan (Yard No. 643).

27.4.1931: Registered in the ownership of the Liverpool and North Wales Steamship Co. Ltd., Liverpool as ST. SEIRIOL.

6.9.1961: Final voyage.

9.11.1962: Register closed on sale to Belgium.

13.11.1962: Left the Mersey under tow of the Dutch tug EBRO having been sold to Van Heyghen Frères A.G., Ghent for £12,000 for breaking up.

22.11.1962: Demolition began.

Top: *St. Seiriol* photographed off the end of Llandudno Pier by Basil Feilden. *[J. & M. Clarkson collection]*

Middle: Docking at Birkenhead. *[M.Cooper/J. & M. Clarkson collection]*

Bottom: Arriving in Douglas, Isle of Man with the *Ben-My-Chree* of 1928 in the background. *[V. E. Barford/Author's collection]*

49

Above: *St. Seiriol* outward bound in the Mersey passing Formby Point. *[Author's collection]*
Below left: *St. Seiriol.* *[Ambrose Greenway collection]*
Below right: *St. Seiriol* passing under the Menai suspension bridge. *[Gwynedd Archives]*

**12. ST. SILIO/ST. TRILLO (2) 1936-
1963 Steel twin-screw motor vessel**
O.N. 164287 314g 122n 149.2 x 27.1 x
10.0 feet
Call sign: MLKL.
Oil engine 2SCSA 12-cyl. by Crossley
Brothers Ltd., Stockport; 13 knots; 223
NHP.

24.3.1936: Launched by the Fairfield
Shipbuilding and Engineering Co. Ltd.,
Govan (Yard No. 657).
16.4.1936: Registered in the ownership of
the Liverpool and North Wales Steamship
Co. Ltd., Liverpool as the ST. SILIO.
23.11.1945: Renamed ST. TRILLO.
2.3.1963: Sold to Townsend Brothers

Ferries Ltd., Coventry, chartered to P. and
A. Campbell Ltd., Cardiff, and continued
to operate short cruises from Llandudno
Pier.
1969: Laid up the end of the summer.
30.10.1972: Sold to Nigel A. Wait, Horne,
Surrey.
1974: Broken up at Dublin.

Above: *St. Silio* off the Liverpool landing stage. *[B. & A. Feilden/J. & M. Clarkson collection]*
Below: *St. Silio* after having her name changed to *St. Trillo*. *[Ambrose Greenway collection]*

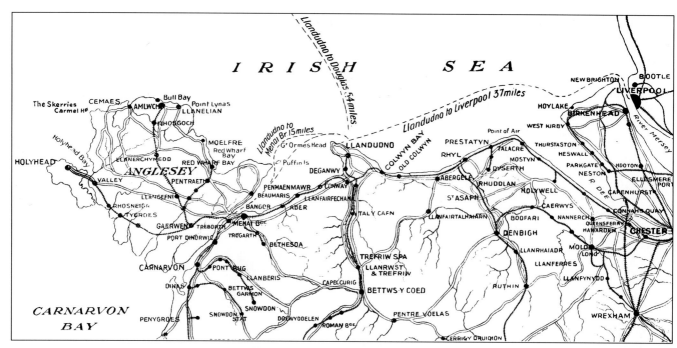

Map of North Wales showing steamer routes of the Liverpool and North Wales Steamship Co. Ltd. taken from a 1950s company guide.

POINTS OF INTEREST ALONG THE WAY

Postcards of piers and other landmarks incorporating ships of the Liverpool and North Wales Steamship Co. Ltd.

Unless indicated otherwise all are from the collection of Ken Saunders.

A busy day on the Princes Landing Stage at Liverpool. From left to right we see the *St. Seiriol* with passengers boarding, three Alexandra tugs, Canadian Pacific's *Empress of Scotland* and in the distance an Isle of Man steamer. A bunkering barge lies in mid-river.

Llandudno Pier and Happy Valley from the air. *St. Seiriol* lies at the pier head.

Right: Llandudno Pier from the landward end with *Snowdon* departing.

Below: St. Seiriol passing Great Orme's Head.

Bystanders watch as *St. Tudno* passes Beaumaris.

Garth Pier, Bangor with *Snowdon* approaching and Anglesey in the background.

BANGOR. THE PIER.

30777

The Menai Straits with the motor vessel *St. Trillo* approaching Normal College, now part of Bangor University.

MENAI STRAITS: MV "ST TRILLO" APPROACHING NORMAL COLLEGE, BANGOR.

St. Tudno at Menai Bridge Pier.

ST. TUDNO AT MENAI BRIDGE PIER.   74805

Telford's suspension bridge over the Menai Straits. The village of Menai Bridge and the pier, with *St. Tudno* alongside, can be seen to the right of the bridge support.

TELFORD'S SUSPENSION BRIDGE, MENAI STRAITS, NORTH WALES.

St. Seiriol and the Britannia Railway Bridge. *[Ambrose Greenway collection]*

Caernarvon Pier with *Snowdon* berthed alongside.

St. Seiriol emerges from behind South Stack on a trip around Anglesey.

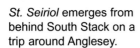
S.13. THE "ST. SEIRIOL" PASSING SOUTH STACK LIGHTHOUSE, HOLYHEAD.

M.V. "ST. SILIO" AT AMLWCH.

Raphael Tuck & Sons, L'
London.

One of a series of photographs produced as picture postcards by Raphael Tuck & Sons Ltd., of the *St. Silio* berthed at Amlwch. Taken on 5th August 1936 this was perhaps her first visit to the port. A big ship for such a small port.

St. Tudno, seen from Penmon Point on Anglesey, passes Puffin Island.

The homeward bound *St. Tudno* passes Penmaenmawr and Llanfairfechan.

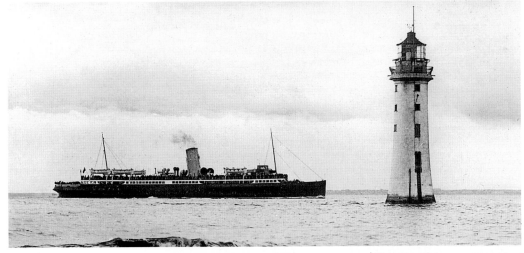

Almost home. *St. Tudno* heading for Liverpool passes the Rock Lighthouse off New Brighton.

The Bay, Douglas, Isle of Man. *St. Seiriol* is berthed in Douglas harbour on one of her day trips to the island. For company she has at least five Isle of Man Steam Packet ships. The Douglas Head ferry lies ahead of her and the stern of a steam dredger is in the bottom left foreground.

FLAGS AND FUNNELS

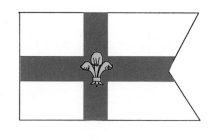

Funnel 1891 to 1904, flag 1891 to 1905.

Funnel 1904 to 1963, flag 1905 to 1963

POSTCARDS TO SEND HOME

Picture postcards were first published towards the end of the nineteenth century and from then on their popularity grew for a number of years both as a collectable item and as a means of sending short messages home to friends and relations. The earliest cards were often artist drawn with undivided backs and a space below the picture for a message. As time went by postcards evolved from drawings to black and white photographs (real photographic cards), to commercially printed black and white cards, sometimes hand coloured, and finally to coloured postcards, both artist drawn and photographic.

The Liverpool and North Wales company published cards for sale on their ships and through outlets ashore whilst other publishers produced cards to sell wherever possible.

The selection reproduced on the following pages illustrates the variety of cards which have been available over the years. All are from the collection of Ken Saunders.

An artist drawn card, with an undivided back, featuring the *St. Tudno* (1) .

Captioned *Last Steamer of the Season, Llandudno*. The ship is *St. Elvies.* No publisher is shown and the card was posted at Pwllheli in 1906.

North Wales, S.S. Snowdon. A Peacock Stylechrom postcard by The Pictorial Stationery Co. Ltd., London.

A Peacock composite card showing *La Marguerite*, *St. Tudno* (1), *St. Elvies* (1), and *Snowdon*. The company's houseflag is in the centre. Again, black and white photographs which have been coloured.

The card, dated 19th August 1908, was sent from 40, Chapel Street, the company's Liverpool office, to Messrs W.H. Parry at Bootle advising them that the September sailing bills had been sent to them by Globe Express 'for your usual attention'.

Llandudno   S. S. "St. Tudno" arriving.

Llandudno S.S. St. Tudno arriving. A postally used card with an undivided back sent to a Miss Grace Hind at Leicester. Again a Peacock card.

Llandudno
La Marguerite.
The card has not been postally used so there is no indication of when published. However, the black paddle boxes would indicate the picture relates to her early years as they were later painted white.

S.S. La Marguerite.
Later in her career with white paddle boxes and with a reproduction of the company's houseflag in the top left corner. This impressive view of her was by C.W. Hunt & Co., Liverpool.

Menai Bridge, the Pier and La Marguerite.
The postmark on the card is 21st August 1905. A Peacock card printed in Saxony.

60

T.S. ST. TUDNO

2,326 gross tons   Length 319 ft.   Speed 19 knots.   2,493 passengers.

T.S. St. Tudno.
A card, based on a colour photograph, published by the Liverpool and North Wales Steamship Co. Ltd. and printed by T. Stephenson and Sons Ltd. at Prescot.

T.S. St. Seiriol.
Dated September 8th 1953 the writer has sent this card along with pictures of two other company ships and some local views to a friend. He tells about crossing on the *St. Seiriol* in fine sunny weather on a calm sea on the last Douglas trip of the season. This card and that of *St. Trillo* below are from paintings by marine artist John Nicholson and would have been commissioned by the company.

T.S. ST. SEIRIOL

1,586 Gross Tons.   Length 269 ft.   Speed 18½ knots.   1,556 Passengers.

M.V. ST. TRILLO

314 Gross Tons.   Length 149 ft.   Speed 12 knots.   568 Passengers.

M.V. St. Trillo.
A company card on this occasion printed by the well known postcard producers J. Salmon Ltd. of Sevenoaks. The card was formerly owned by the artist J. Nicholson and bears his signature and address.

THE OFFICIAL GUIDES

Most years, war years excepted, a guide book *North Wales Coast, Official Guide of The Liverpool & North Wales Steamship Company Ltd.* was produced for sale on board the ships and through various outlets on shore. The publisher of the earlier guides was W.H.Evans & Sons Ltd. of Chester. In the 1920s the publisher was Littlebury Bros. Ltd., of Liverpool and Manchester. In later issues the Liverpool and North Wales Steamship Co. Ltd. becomes the publisher in the 1950s with T. Stephenson and Sons Ltd., Prescot as printers. The 1901 guide was priced at twopence (less than 1p) without a map or threepence with a map. By the thirty-fifth edition in 1953, the price had risen to sixpence, or just 2.5 pence.

The contents varied somewhat but all earlier editions contained advertisements for guest houses and hotels, along with restaurants, bars and public houses in Liverpool and the North Wales resorts. Adverts for establishments inland and ways of getting there were also featured. The ships in the current fleet were described and sometimes illustrated with external and internal views. In later years a simple fleet list was included. Distance tables, sailing schedules, fares and details of how to get to the ships were clearly laid out as were the company's conditions of carriage. From the 1930s onwards a brief history of The Fairfield Shipbuilding and Engineering Co. Ltd. - builders of the *St. Tudno, St. Seiriol* and *St. Silio* was included. Most of each guide was taken up by details of what the different ports of call had to offer in the way of entertainment and attractions.

Over the years seven different designs were used for the covers of the original guides - each reflecting the style of the period in which they appreared. No indication is given of the designer, no doubt all were prepared in house by the publishers.

Editions 1 and 2: The Menai Bridge and the *St. Tudno* (1), used for the first two known editions of the guide in the years 1901 to 1903.

Editions 3 to 10, 1904 to 1911. Illustrated with the Menai Bridge but now with the *La Marguerite*, new to the company in 1904.

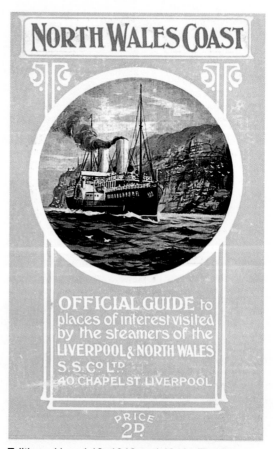

Editions 11 and 12, 1912 and 1913. The *La Marguerite* sails on with the Great Orme in the background.

Editions 13 to 16, 1914 to 1925. The suspension of services during the Great War resulted in fewer guides being produced in this period, however the very popular *La Marguerite* remains prominent.

Editions 17 to 30, 1926 to 1939. *La Marguerite*, scrapped in 1925, has now been replaced by *St. Tudno*, new in 1926. The 1939 edition continued in use up to and including the 1948 season.

Editions 31 to 34, 1949 to 1952. After the break for the Second World War the first new cover design appeared in 1949. *St. Tudno* sails on with a more contemporary background.

Editions 35 and 36, 1953 to 1955. The last versions of the "North Wales Coast". By now passenger numbers were declining and expenses would be cut back where ever possible.

Right: The Sea Route from Liverpool to North Wales
At least six versions of this guide were produced in the period 1956 to 1959. All were almost identical with the same view of *St. Tudno*.

Below: A third type of guide produced by the company was Picturesque North Wales, the favourite route. A cheaper version, perhaps for giving away with tickets, and half the size of the other guides measuring only 12 x 10cms. Made up of twenty four pages the contents were similar to the others but much briefer and without adverts. The two illustrated are dated 1931 (left) and 1949.

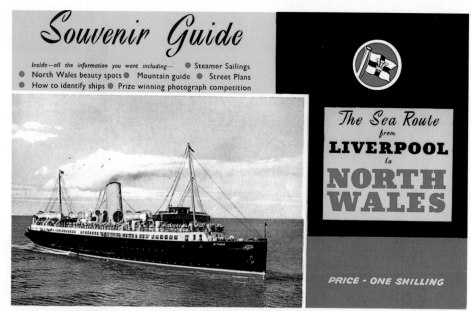

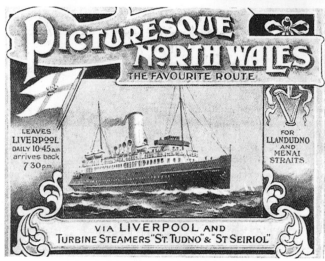

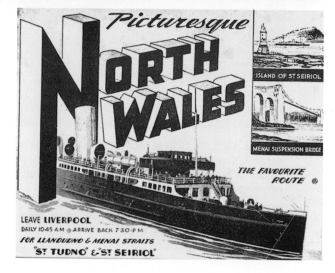

INDEX